FIGS

Edible

Series Editor: Andrew F. Smith

EDIBLE is a revolutionary series of books dedicated to food and drink that explores the rich history of cuisine. Each book reveals the global history and culture of one type of food or beverage.

Already published

Apple Erika Janik *Barbecue* Jonathan Deutsch and Megan J. Elias *Beef* Lorna Piatti-Farnell *Beer* Gavin D. Smith *Brandy* Becky Sue Epstein *Bread* William Rubel *Cake* Nicola Humble *Caviar* Nichola Fletcher *Champagne* Becky Sue Epstein *Cheese* Andrew Dalby *Chocolate* Sarah Moss and Alexander Badenoch *Cocktails* Joseph M. Carlin *Curry* Colleen Taylor Sen *Dates* Nawal Nasrallah *Eggs* Diane Toops *Figs* David C. Sutton *Game* Paula Young Lee *Gin* Lesley Jacobs Solmonson *Hamburger* Andrew F. Smith *Herbs* Gary Allen *Hot Dog* Bruce Kraig *Ice Cream* Laura B. Weiss *Lemon* Toby Sonneman *Lobster* Elisabeth Townsend *Milk* Hannah Velten *Mushroom* Cynthia D. Bertelsen *Nuts* Ken Albala *Offal* Nina Edwards *Olive* Fabrizia Lanza *Oranges* Clarissa Hyman *Pancake* Ken Albala *Pie* Janet Clarkson *Pineapple* Kaori O' Connor *Pizza* Carol Helstosky *Pork* Katharine M. Rogers *Potato* Andrew F. Smith *Rice* Renee Marton *Rum* Richard Foss *Salmon* Nicolaas Mink *Sandwich* Bee Wilson *Sauces* Maryann Tebben *Soup* Janet Clarkson *Spices* Fred Czarra *Tea* Helen Saberi *Whiskey* Kevin R. Kosar *Wine* Marc Millon

Figs
A Global History

David C. Sutton

REAKTION BOOKS

For Deborah, naturally

Published by Reaktion Books Ltd
33 Great Sutton Street
London EC1V 0DX, UK
www.reaktionbooks.co.uk

First published 2014

Printed and bound in China
by Toppan Printing Co. Ltd

A catalogue record for this book is available
from the British Library

ISBN 978 1 78023 349 9

Contents

Introducing the Fig

The fig is a deliciously flavoured, very soft and seedy fruit which can be consumed in various forms: fresh, canned, bottled and, above all, dried. The fresh fig is regarded as a luxury fruit, sometimes the supreme luxury fruit, even in countries where it grows abundantly. The dried fig is rather more humble, and has long been a staple food in Mediterranean countries – in ancient Rome it was used to feed the marching armies, as a substitute for bread. Of all the figs harvested in the world, over 85 per cent are dried and over 10 per cent canned or bottled, while only about 3 per cent are eaten fresh.

The fig is the fruit of the common fig tree (*Ficus carica*), which originated in the Near East, probably somewhere in Arabia. Today the leading fig-growing countries are Turkey and Egypt. The Anatolian heartland of modern Turkey is said to have the perfect climate for the growing of figs. Figs are also an important crop in Greece, Italy, Spain, Portugal and California. Although they grow mostly in the northern hemisphere, figs also thrive in Peru, Argentina, South Africa and Australia.

Figs were loved and worshipped by the ancient Greeks and Romans, but they remained particular to the Mediterranean and Near East regions until about the twelfth century. In the

Figs are the fruit of late-summer Mediterranean sunshine.

last 800 years the love of figs has spread to many other countries, including northern Europe, where they were often first introduced by returning Crusaders.

The fresh fig is succulent with a distinctive scented flavour, sweet and rich and with several aphrodisiac associations. The classic fresh fig is dark purple or violet when ripe, but some types of fig can also ripen brown or green.

Some species of fig tree will give two or even three crops of fruit. The early summer crop is usually green and is sometimes described as a 'breba' crop. Opinions vary from country to country about the edibility of brebas, but for most fig-lovers the truly wondrous fruits are those which ripen in the late summer or early autumn.

Most fig tree species are self-pollinating (or partheno-carpic), but some are not. These latter require the wriggling and squirming intervention of tiny insects known as a fig wasps or blastophaga. Self-pollinating figs are referred to as Adriatic

Jacques Le Moyne de Morgues, *Ficus carica*, a fine 16th-century drawing of fig leaves and fruit.

Dried figs are different from fresh in both appearance and use. They are a fruit of winter sustenance, a winter luxury for the poor.

Luis Egidio Meléndez, *Still-life with Figs and Bread*, 1760s, oil on canvas, showing green and black figs which are ripe to bursting.

figs, while those requiring the assistance of insects to ripen are often called Smyrna figs. Adriatic figs are commoner, and the principal cultivars include 'Brown Turkey', 'Brunswick', 'Celeste', 'Kadota', 'White Adriatic' and 'Black Mission'. Two of the primary characteristics of Smyrna figs are their dependence on fig wasps and the fact that they do not usually produce brebas. According to the Californian fig expert W. B. Storey, the finest fig grown in California, which still bears its original Turkish name, 'Sari Lop', is of the Smyrna type.

Although the fig tree is normally grown for its fruit, it is also a fine ornamental tree and may be grown in more northern regions – where the fruit will not ripen – for what the Royal Horticultural Society, in a striking phrase, calls its 'beautiful architectural foliage'.

In the Western world, the most familiar introduction to the fig comes in the opening pages of the Bible, where we read

Made notorious by the story of the Garden of Eden, the fig leaf has its own distinctive beauty.

that Adam and Eve in the Garden of Eden used some of that architectural foliage to cover themselves when they became aware of their nakedness. Today the term 'fig leaf' is often used as a metaphor for a (usually futile) attempt to conceal something potentially embarrassing.

I

The Fruit of Paradise

Figs are the fruit of Paradise. This chapter looks at figs in two different types of paradise: first, the religious Paradise Lost, the biblical Garden of Eden, and second, the more modern conception of paradise as a dreamland of luxury and exotic delights, peopled by voluptuaries, libertines and lovers of the finest foods.

For many people, figs have biblical connotations. In the resounding language of the Authorized Version of Genesis (3:6–7), we read:

> And when the woman saw that the tree was good for food, and that it was pleasant to the eyes, and a tree to be desired to make one wise, she took of the fruit thereof, and did eat, and gave also unto her husband with her, and he did eat.
>
> And the eyes of them both were opened, and they knew that they were naked; and they sewed fig leaves together and made themselves aprons.

It is a curiosity of Christian iconography through the centuries that while the leaves of Paradise are clearly defined as fig leaves, the fruit (unspecified in the Bible) is usually depicted as an apple.

So before we move on to consider botany and history, let us first restore the fig to its rightful position as the fruit of the biblical Paradise. The fruit which tempted Eve and which she plucked in the Garden of Eden should be interpreted not as an apple but as a fig. The evidence and the arguments for this are clear. The early Genesis stories, up until the flood of Noah, derive from the traditions of Mesopotamia. Although apples do grow in central Iraq (the sociologist and food historian Sami Zubaida told me there was an apple tree in the Baghdad garden of his childhood), they are rare, small and untempting, whereas figs ripen to sweet perfection in Mesopotamia. The Bible is clear that there were fig trees in the Garden of Eden; apples are not mentioned. Figs are the fruit of temptation, lusciously alluring. Apples are all very well, but not notable enough, surely, to

Prepared in a rich sauce of wine or honey, this is the taste of paradise in a bowl.

Pierre Auguste Renoir (1841–1919), *Apricots and Figs*, oil on canvas.

tempt a woman into original sin. And fig trees are more 'pleasant to the eyes' than apple trees. Meanwhile, figs are associated with Paradise in other religions – the prophet Muhammad is quoted as saying: 'If I should wish one fruit brought to paradise, it would certainly be the fig.' Fig leaves from the fruit tree can indeed be sewn with a needle and thread. There is no need to surmise – as Milton proposed in *Paradise Lost* – that the tree in question was some sort of Indian banyan and 'not that kind for fruit renowned'.

Indeed, there are some interpretations that do suggest the forbidden fruit was a fig, though they are less well known than those favouring the apple. The apple may be a northern European superimposition. Notably, dictionaries of fable and folklore describe the fig tree as 'the tree of wisdom, vigour and creation'.

Part of the frieze from Notre-Dame in Paris, showing Adam and Eve and the serpent entwined in a fig tree. So is the forbidden fruit an apple or a fig?

The Biblical Fig

We should look a little more closely at the biblical fig, because it is a rewarding and sometimes surprising theme. The Bible might not commonly be associated with fables about talking trees, for example, but we find one such story in the Book of Judges, in which the fig tree is portrayed as possessing a wisdom based on its place in the natural order:

> Then the trees said to the fig tree, 'You come and be our king!' The fig tree replied 'Must I forgo my sweetness, forgo my excellent fruit, to go and hold sway over the trees?'

Whether you read this as a melancholy reflection on the task of being a ruler, or favour another of the multiple interpret - ations the exchange is subject to, one thing is clear, and that is the biblical primacy of the fig tree.

The fig also plays an emblematic role in several Palestine-specific sequences of the Bible. When spies return to report on Canaan as the 'promised land' (Numbers 13:23) they bring with them grapes, pomegranates and figs; elsewhere the land promised to the Israelites is described (Deuteronomy 8:8) as a good land, of wheat and barley and vines and fig trees and pomegranates. The fig has a similar prominence in the Song of Songs:

> Flowers are appearing on the earth,
> The season of glad songs has come,
> The cooing of the turtledove is heard in our land,
> The fig tree is forming its first figs
> And the blossoming vines give out their fragrance.

Meanwhile, when Abigail went out to meet King David, a man of great and sometimes dubious appetites, she offered him a hundred clusters of raisins and two hundred cakes of figs (1 Samuel 25:18).

Of the many references to figs in the Old Testament, these are three of the most attractive:

> But they shall sit every man under his vine and under his fig tree; and none shall make them afraid. (Micah 4:4)

> All thy strong holds shall be like fig trees with the first-ripe figs: if they be shaken, they shall even fall into the mouth of the eater. (Nahum 3:12)

And Judah and Israel dwelt safely, every man under his vine and under his fig tree, from Dan even to Beersheba, all the days of Solomon. (1 Kings 4:25)

Particular importance was attached in Jewish thinking to the idea of sitting under a fig tree. There is a story in the New Testament (in St John's Gospel) of a man called Nathanael who appears to be converted to Jesus' cause simply because Jesus had spotted him sitting under a fig tree. This story is variously interpreted by Christian and Jewish scholars, but there is a shared view that sitting under a fig tree is associated with devout study of the Torah. The shadowy ancient image of Nathanael under the fig tree on the wall of the historic Sinagoga Santa María La Blanca in Toledo is captioned 'Nathanael under the fig tree, which symbolises the study of the Torah'.

Another puzzling fig story from the New Testament is told by St Mark:

And seeing a fig tree afar off having leaves, he came, if haply he might find any thing thereon: and when he came to it, he found nothing but leaves; for the time of figs was not yet.

And Jesus answered and said unto it, No man eat fruit of thee hereafter for ever. And his disciples heard it.

It is hard to see what the fig tree had done wrong. The time of figs comes later than the time of other fruit; fig trees never bear fruit in early spring and often not even at the height of summer. We will consider later the influence of this strange Gospel story on the English tradition of figgy pudding.

Earthly Paradise

Let us turn, though, from religion to more earthly forms of paradise: delight, luxury and sweetness. In the world of food and cookery, images of paradise frequently lead to thoughts of preparing and eating figs. One of the words most often used in fig recipes is 'luscious', and figs can draw even the most practical of food writers into a universe of excess. A wonderful Elizabeth David recipe, for duck with figs, begins by advising the reader to put sixteen fresh figs into a half bottle of Sauternes for 24 hours.

In similar mood, the French chef Gaston Lenôtre created a sorbet of Muscat de Rivesaltes with figs and mint, which requires a whole bottle of chilled Muscat. *Larousse Gastronomique* recommends that braised pheasant should be stuffed with dried figs which have been soaked in generous quantities of port for 24 hours, while Diana Henry, in her *Roast Figs, Sugar Snow* (2011), presents a recipe for roast goose

Figs on a plate, emphasizing the special fig shape.

coated with honey, stuffed with chestnuts and dried figs poached in Calvados, and decorated with roasted fresh figs. In 1949, amid rumours of an on-set romance between Ingrid Bergman and Roberto Rossellini during the making of the film *Stromboli, terra di dio*, there emerged a love-salad known as *Insalata Stromboli*, to the delight of actor and director. Its main ingredients were fresh figs, anchovies, fennel, capers, mint and roasted red peppers. Even Delia Smith has been lured into the extravagance of a compote of fresh figs in nearly half a litre of Marsala wine with mascarpone mousse; while honey-roasted figs in Marsala presents a combination of rich flavours – a delightful Sicilian classic found in several recipe collections.

Maria Sibylla Merian, watercolour drawing of a goldfinch on the branch of a fig tree, *c.* 1693–1700.

Near to the town of Higuera de la Sierra in Huelva, Spain (named because it lies among the fig groves in the mountains), you may be served chocolate-coated dried figs in a creamy sauce flavoured with the local acorn liqueur (*licor de bellota de la Sierra de Aracena*). Further south in Huelva province, you might be fortunate enough to be offered honeyed fresh figs poached in oloroso sherry – another divine mix of flavours.

A more aromatic approach is found in the Israeli recipes which slowly stew fresh figs in a sauce of red wine flavoured with honey, thyme, bay leaves and cinnamon, while for those who prefer the classic flavour of the ripe fig without the stickiness of honey, the Lebanese preference for walking slowly in the late summer sunshine while eating figs and drinking iced arak (an anise-flavoured spirit) with fresh mint leaves provides a perfect activity for a sunny Mediterranean afternoon. Aniseed, mint and figs make another classic gastronomic combination, while a similar modern Maltese delicacy is made by steeping newly dried figs in aniseed liqueur, mixed with fennel seed and bay leaves.

There is something very special, and redolent of an earthly paradise, about walking in a garden in the late summer, talking with friends while drinking flavoured alcohol and eating figs. Here is Samuel Pepys on 21 July 1662:

> Thence to the dock, where we walked in Mr Shelden's garden. Eating more fruit, and drinking, and eating figs, which were very good, and talking while the 'Regal James' was bringing towards the dock . . .

As for excess, we have the example of the fig-lovers of Kabylie in northern Algeria. Several sources describe how the Kabyles would eat figs until they became intoxicated and would then engage in drunken, weaving dances. A now-rare book entitled *En Kabylie: voyage d'une parisienne au Djujura* (1875) contains descriptions of fig feasting and fig drunkenness, which the author (a woman writing under the name J. Vilbort) describes as neither gross nor wicked but rather as an exalted love of liberty. One Kabyle woman told Madame Vilbort,

> Drunkenness on wine is unknown to us, but we do know drunkenness on figs. At the time of the fig harvest, on the lovely autumn evenings, it always happens that the harvesters become drunk from eating so many of these rich fruit, and above all from talking, laughing and frolicking in the midst of all the abundance.

Ira J. Condit, a great authority on figs who was writing over 60 years ago, calculated that an average family of Kabyles would consume 1500 lb (680 kg) of figs a year.

The Kabyles also had a love of alcohol derived from figs (regardless of their conversion to Islam, which was thought to be nominal); their version was usually described as a fig brandy. We also find the expressions 'fig wine' and 'fig alcohol' in historical works about strong drink. Fig alcohols found in countries including Morocco, Tunisia and Mallorca are usually rich, dark brown and sticky-sweet, and all too moreish. It is rare for one glass not to be followed by another.

In Tunisia there is also a fig brandy called *boukha* (*eau de vie de figues*), a commercial version of which is now being sold as Boukha Soleil. In Morocco there is a date and fig liqueur known as *mahia*. Expatriates in Nice have begun to produce a delightful variant called *mahia meknesiah*, which is fig brandy flavoured with aniseed.

Readers who are tempted to seek out and try Boukha Soleil or *mahia meknesiah* are recommended also to look for a novel alcohol of figs and juniper berries known as figuette. But be

Consume with caution. Fig brandy, usually known as *boukha*, is another form of temptation.

aware: figuette is often found in non-alcoholic form – very refreshing and delicious but nevertheless . . . non-alcoholic.

The Turkish-Balkan firewater raki is another drink usually flavoured with aniseed and is a much harsher spirit. It may be made, especially in rural areas, from figs as well as from grapes. In southern Turkey fig raki (known as *incir rakisi*) is said to send people to bed happy and to provoke sweet dreams.

Fig wine had been known in ancient Iraq and ancient Egypt, and had been especially appreciated in ancient Rome, where Apicius and others called it *caricarum*, from a type of fig called Carica. Sotion, the teacher of Seneca, is said to have recommended wine made from green figs. Even more than wine from grapes, in these ancient societies fig wine was associated with dancing, frolicking and cavorting.

To conclude this review of the earthly paradise, here is an ancient Egyptian vision of heaven on earth, in a story collected by the scholar E. A. Wallis Budge:

> This beautiful region was called Aa. In it there are figs, and wine is more abundant than water. Honey is plentiful, oil exists in large quantities, and fruits of every kind are on the trees. Wheat, barley, herds of cattle, and flocks of sheep and goats are there in untold numbers.

Egypt has always been one of the leading lands of figs, and, as we shall see, in the twenty-first century it remains second only to Turkey in fig production. What we notice here, however, is that the first-named component of the paradise of Aa is the fig.

2

A Botanical Curiosity

The edible fig is a freak of botany. The modern fig tree (*Ficus carica*) is a descendant of the wild caprifig, modified by human intervention. Caprifig trees do produce a form of fruit, which can (just about) be eaten, but caprifigs look and taste wizened and unimpressive. The *Ficus* genus is part of the wider family known as Moraceae, which means that figs form part of the same family as mulberries and breadfruit.

Fig trees are juicy and aromatic and often beautifully shaped. They are fine trees to sit under. When cut, the branches ooze a white sap which can be an irritant on the skin. The bark and the wood are attractive to rodents and rabbits, while the soft fruit is especially vulnerable to birds. In traditional cultures, scaring small animals away from the fig trees was a pleasant job for children.

Edible figs were first developed probably around 6,000 years ago, when a number of other wild fruit products began to be improved as part of the development of human civilization.

Spanish dictionaries define the fig as the second of two fruits of the fig tree. The first fruit they describe with the word *breva*. Like caprifigs, these early-fruiting brevas (sometimes found in English, though not in the *Oxford English Dictionary*, as 'brebas') can be eaten, but they are often better baked or

Ripe and unripe figs grow together on the same tree.

stewed. Raw, they may taste unripe. In France, brebas are known as *figue-fleurs* and, at least in Toulouse, are not generally considered edible. In Spanish Catalonia (where they are known as *figaflor* or *bacora*) and in Italy (known as *fioroni*), by contrast, they are considered not only edible but delicious. Catalan sources point out that Plato preferred brebas to figs, and that Galen recommended brebas to competitors in the Olympic Games as ideal food for athletes. Italian sources describe the *fiorone verde dottato* as a small green fruit with a pink interior which is delightfully sweet.

Clearly, however, there is some confusion between figs and brebas in common parlance. Often the fruit known as 'green fig' will in fact be a form of breba. In the version of Catalan spoken in the fig-rich island of Menorca, *figaflor* is not regarded as a breba but as the earliest fruiting of all the varieties of fig, while in Ischia in Italy they prize a fruit known as *fiorone nero* (black breba), a black fruit with pink flesh which has a reputation for keeping and travelling well. This must surely

Ripe brebas. Plato was said to have preferred spring brebas to late-summer figs. Many Catalonians would agree with him.

also be an early cropping fig. There is certainly confusion in the *Larousse Gastronomique*. My own edition states, with typical confidence, that there are three types of fig: the white fig, the purple fig and the red fig. This categorical assertion is accompanied by a captioned photograph of a green fig.

Black or purple figs are known to be 'dominant' over white or green figs. This is demonstrated by the fact that when a black strain is cross-bred with a white strain, the resulting hybrid is always black.

While most Spanish varieties of fig do indeed have two crops, this is not universal. There are single-crop fig varieties which fruit early – like the Menorcan *figaflor* – and there are, more usually, single-crop fig varieties which fruit late, in the northern hemisphere in September or October. Most trees in Turkey are single-cropping, and the Turkish language does not distinguish between figs and brebas, both being covered by the word *incir*. There are also, remarkably, especially in Italy, fig trees which bear three crops. The early Italian crop is the *fioroni*; the main fig crop *fichi* or *forniti*; and the third crop is known as *cimaruoli*.

The fruit nestling in its leaves.

The fig wasp in close-up. The similarity to the garden wasp is very slight.

This multi-cropping is very unusual among fruits. But, botanically, the fig is stranger than that. To begin with, it is not strictly a fruit at all, but rather a tiny cluster of ingrowing flowers; second, many species of fig tree require the pollinating intervention of tiny fig wasps or blastophaga before they can fruit at all; and third, the fig is the only fruit tree which does not produce a display of blossom in the weeks before the fruit begins to form. The Chinese word for fig translates as 'fruit without a flower'.

Commentators tend to say that the fig is 'neither fruit nor flower', but a little of both. The technical word for the fig's pattern of growth is 'inflorescence', meaning flowering inwards. The tiny flowers never bloom, of course, because they never see the light, but they ripen inwards and the ripened little seeds and their coating become something which is popularly known as the sweetest of fruits.

As mentioned in the Introduction, the two principal types of fig are often distinguished as Adriatic figs and Smyrna figs. Adriatic figs often produce brebas; they are usually self-pollinating, and hence easier to grow. Unfortunately, there is a widespread belief that Smyrna figs, especially those of genuine Turkish origin, taste better. It is regarded as a truism that the

Unripe green figs, taking their special shape before ripening.

finest figs grown in California are the Smyrna figs known as 'Sari Lop'. Smyrna figs do not usually bear brebas and will only bear ripe fruit if they have been pollinated by fig wasps, in a process known as 'caprification'. Caprification is the transfer of caprifig pollen to the ingrowing flowers of immature figs by the introduction of fig wasps. In peasant cultures over many centuries the fig wasps were first introduced to pollen-bearing caprifigs, and then inserted into the figs by hand.

So the expression 'freak of botany' is no exaggeration. We are dealing with fruit from multi-cropping trees, which are not really fruit at all but a form of ingrowing flower in a ribbed and skin-like case, and which often depend upon a strange little insect in order to be fertilized and to thrive. The fig is also dependent upon particular forms of climate and environment: it is intolerant of frost and even of cold weather; it likes hot weather but not damp heat, although a very slight dampening when the crop is almost formed can be beneficial. Fig trees are superbly resistant to drought.

It is sometimes said, especially by Turkish writers, that the ideal climate for the ripening of figs is to be found in the valley of the winding Meander river (Homer's Skamander, known as Büyük Menderes in modern Turkey – our word 'meander' derives from its name). The Meander valley has hot and dry summers, with temperatures regularly rising above 40°C. During June and July, baking, dry winds come from the north and enable the fruit to move towards perfect ripeness, before the winds turn westerly and slightly damper in August, allowing the ripe figs to plump out without over-drying.

Figs also grow well in desert oases, where they are suited to the combination of hot sun and groundwater. In his *Travels in Syria and the Holy Land*, John Lewis Burckhardt (1784–1817) describes the Arabian settlement of Tebouk:

> One day from Dzat Hadj is Tebouk, a castle, with a vil-
> lage of Felahein, of the tribe of Arabs Hammeide. There
> is a copious source of water, and gardens of figs and
> pomegranate trees, where Badintshaus, onions and other
> vegetables are also cultivated.

Other climates which are especially favourable for ripe fig crops are those of North Africa (notably Algeria); the Mediterranean islands (Cyprus, Crete, Chios, the Cyclades, Malta, Sicily and Pantelleria, Mallorca, Menorca, Ibiza, Corsica); the Lebanon, Israel and Palestine; Syria and the Crimean part of Russia; Yemen and Iraq, where, as we shall see, cultivated figs originated; Peru, Mexico and parts of California.

CEVİZ
OVA

Choosing the best: at the main market in Istanbul.

3
Origins in Arabia and Mesopotamia

Like many things which add value or delight to human life (art, music, dance, architecture, cookery and recipes, literature, gardening, wine, decoration, mathematics, metalworking, astronomy, medicine, even banking), the pleasure of eating figs derives from Iraq.

Cultivated figs became a major feature of the first great human civilization in Mesopotamia. They did not, however, originate there. Most of the dependable sources for archaeology and fruit history indicate that figs were first cultivated in southern Arabia. It is an interesting corrective to some modern Western prejudices to reflect that the fig, that most exquisite and civilized of cultivated fruit, very likely started out with a journey from Yemen to Iraq.

To return briefly to the Mesopotamian origins of the early part of the Book of Genesis, it is apposite to recall that some archaeologists, following Geoffrey Bibby, have sought to locate the pre-Mesopotamian civilization of Dilmun, and the principal suggested locations are Bahrain and Yemen. If there were a real historical figure behind the biblical Adam, and if the first ruler of the Mesopotamian Eden had journeyed there with his followers from Dilmun, it would be romantic to speculate that King Adam may have brought figs and fig trees with him.

A classic scene from Arab lands: the seller of dried figs, with his figs piled on a blanket.

This would certainly be a more attractive story than the usual prosaic archaeological explanation, which is that the earliest fig seeds probably travelled from Yemen to Iraq, borne there inside the dung of animals such as dromedaries and asses.

Botanists generally agree with archaeologists as to the origins of the fig. Most botanical texts describe the fig as indigenous to Asia Minor, Iran and Syria, with a secondary spread to the whole Mediterranean region. Botanists who are prepared to be more specific will indicate that fig trees probably originated in the Arabian peninsula – evolving, thanks to human intervention, from caprifigs – and began to be cultivated as an edible fruit in Mesopotamia well over 5,000 years ago. Some will go as far as 6,000 years ago, or slightly more. The working consensus is that the fig evolved and developed in southern Arabia and was then improved by Sumerian and Assyrian fruit farmers before becoming a mainstream crop across Iraq, Greater Syria and Anatolia.

It is therefore surprising that the great historian Herodotus of Halicarnassus (usually thought of as Greek, but actually from fig-rich Anatolia) stated that the people of the Tigris region had no knowledge of figs. This can be true only if his remarks were referring solely to the mountain warriors from the north of modern Iraq. Figs were certainly known in the ancient cities of Babylon and Nineveh. The Sumerian king Urukagina, who ruled about 2900 BC, mentioned figs in his stone writings and referred to their medicinal properties. And a Babylonian hymn-book which has been dated to around 2000 BC uses the phrase 'sweeter than dates or figs'. The limited written record therefore supports the archaeological evidence, and scholars have also reported artistic representations of figs. Fig leaves and fruit have been identified in designs on Assyrian monuments, and artistic representations of ancient Nineveh also show cultivated fig trees growing.

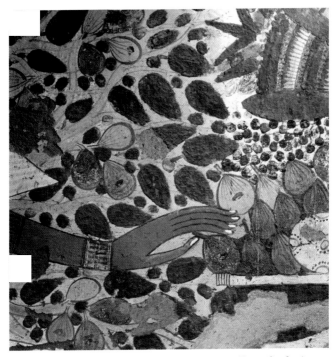

An elegant Egyptian hand snakes forward to help itself to a fig: figs in an Egyptian wall painting.

The consensual, if tentative, time and place for the origins of cultivated figs – 4000 BC or a little later in Arabia and Mesopotamia – were recently challenged. In 2006 a report appeared in *Science* magazine suggesting that remains of carbonized cultivated figs had been discovered by archaeologists working on the Gilgal I site, a Neolithic village in the Jordan Valley. This 'discovery' was fairly precisely dated to around 9300 BC. The extraordinarily early date for fruit cultivation potentially overturned all existing ideas about human horticulture and attracted widespread news coverage, on the BBC and elsewhere. Later in 2006, however, unnoticed by the news media, another group of scientists published a refutation in *Science*, proposing that what had been found were not Neolithic cultivated figs (against all probability) but unpollinated female spring figs. These were described by the scientists as brebas, but we could also characterize them as caprifigs – the wild proto-figs whose name, meaning 'goat figs', was given to them by the Romans and indicated that they were a food source for wandering desert

Fig trees are renowned for their apparent strength, resilience and determination. This picture shows a fig tree cleaving a great rock at Wadi Shaib, Jordan, 1930s.

scapegoats. This seems to make a lot more sense. Charles M. Doughty, the tireless writer and researcher on the arid lands of 'Arabia Deserta', refers always to 'wild figs' in the descriptions of his travels.

With the present state of archaeological and palaeobotanical research, therefore, we are safest to say that, while caprifigs have been shown to be in existence over 11,000 years ago, the most probable origins for cultivated figs remain in Arabia and Mesopotamia around 6,000 years ago.

Another recent archaeological find which attracted attention to the global history of figs was that at Assos in Turkey. In 2008 it was reported that figs buried in one of the tombs at Assos around 2400 years ago had been found to be edible. The head of the Assos dig, Nurettin Arslan, commented that the figs had probably been placed in the tomb in an unripe state and that was why they had survived to the present day.

This ancient oval basket containing figs and dates, now in the British Museum, was retrieved from the valley of the Nile.

Dried figs at the Berber market of Imilchil, Morocco.

There was restrained speculation in the Turkish press as to whether the figs had been entombed for their nutritional or their aphrodisiac qualities.

Figs in the Ancient Near East

Figs are known to have been of primary importance in the succession of early Near East regimes which mark the beginnings of Western civilization – Sumerian, Babylonian, Assyrian, Hittite, Phrygian, Trojan, Egyptian and Persian – but, in marked contrast to the later regimes in Greece and Rome, written sources are scarce and literary sources almost non-existent. As the Egyptologist Edda Bresciani has lamented, even ancient Egypt has left us no texts comparable to those of the Roman authors Apicius and Pliny. We have to assemble a few sparse scraps and snippets – funerary meals, doctors' prescriptions, lists of foods and even accounts of monarchs' dreams – to add to the archaeological evidence.

For the Sumerian civilization, cuneiform sources identify figs alongside apples, grapes, oil, honey, cheese, onions, leeks and garlic among the basic foodstuffs. And the medical properties of figs were recognized, with one prescription from around 2750 BC including thyme, pears and figs. Similarly, the early Babylonian texts list dates, figs, apples, pomegranates, quince, almonds, pistachio and lotus.

For the Assyrians, we have a few texts by Sargon of Akkad from around 2400 BC. In one, he states that he had brought back figs from Anatolia (modern Turkey). This is usually interpreted to mean that he brought back new Anatolian varieties to add to the ones already known in Assyria. Sargon also claimed to have captured the city of Ebla in Syria. Ebla is still being excavated, but its crops have been found to

Pharaoh Seti offering food to the goddess Hathor.

Figs from the Nile Valley over 3,000 years ago. The fig shape is unmistakable.

include barley, wheat, olives, figs, grapes, pomegranates and flax.

The royal texts of the Hittite city of Ugarit mention a cake baked with dried figs, and Charles Allen Burney's *Historical Dictionary of the Hittites* (2004) tells us that olives, figs and grapes are often found together in Hittite rituals. In one intriguing source, the Hittite queen Puduhepa, who reigned in the thirteenth century BC, reported a strange and worrying dream in which her cheese, figs and raisins had all gone mouldy.

There are all too few written sources for the Phrygians (fewer than fifty inscriptions in total, mostly funerary). The Phrygians were one of the many ancient Mediterranean races, up to and including the Romans, who had a cult of worship of the fig tree. The Greeks were aware of the sweetness and quality of Phrygian dried figs, whilst being ultra-sensitive to issues around products with non-Greek, strange-sounding names. This led to a Greek view that Phrygian figs from the Brigindara region were barbarian in name but Attic in flavour and enjoyment.

For the Trojans, there are no surviving written texts at all, and we cannot even be sure whether their language was closer to Hittite or to Greek. The archaeologist Carl Blegen identified seeds of grain, figs and olives in one of his digs at Hisarlik, the most likely site for Troy. And Michael Wood tells us that characteristic of the Trojan diet were oil, grain, figs and wine.

Egyptian archaeological research places the origins of fig cultivation there around 2750 BC, perhaps a little earlier with the discovery of a dish of stewed figs as part of a Second Dynasty funerary meal at Saqqara. Like the Hittites, the Egyptians are known to have favoured cakes and bread which were baked with figs. There is a fine drawing of a fig harvest in the grave of Khnumhotep at Beni Hasan (around 1900 BC).

The food historian Bernard Rosenberger tells us that in the ancient Arab lands fruit was not regarded as a real foodstuff, but was used for snacks and accompaniments. The two exceptions to this were figs and grapes.

There is no direct written evidence of fig production in ancient Persia, although the *Encyclopaedia Iranica* states that the known fig cultures in contemporary neighbouring Babylonia and Assyria make it certain that Persia also produced figs in very early times. In his wonderful account of an army on the march, *The Persian Expedition*, Xenophon several times records their finding 'plenty of figs' on the route, but this was in Asiatic Thrace, not Persia. Strabo (d. *c.* AD 24) reports on successful fig growing in Hyrcania, just south of the Caspian Sea. The Zoroastrians held that figs were one of the ten kinds of fruit of which both the outside and the inside were edible. And finally, in a bittersweet anecdote which rings true, Xerxes, the king of the Persians, is said to have regularly eaten Attican figs around 470 BC to remind himself exactly why he so wanted to return and reconquer Greece.

This idyllic image shows a fig tree beside the Aegean Sea.

4
Figs in Ancient Greece

Figs were a constant presence in Greek society, with the first Greek cultivation of figs probably occurring around 900 BC on the mainland and many centuries earlier than that on Crete. It appears that figs were already known and venerated at the high period of Cretan culture around 1500 BC. In Greek mythology there was a Titan whose name derived from the word for fig (συκή or *syke*); his name was Sykeus and he was one of the Titans who waged war against Zeus. After the defeat of the Titans, Sykeus took flight and was protected by his mother Gaia (the earth), who transformed him into a fig tree.

In the second generation of myths, there is a story of an Athenian called Phytalus who welcomed the goddess Demeter into his home and was rewarded by her with the gift of the first fig tree. This formula-myth is quite similar to the one which tells of Athena's gift of olives and olive oil to Athens, but the geographer Pausanias says that the fig myth is confirmed by the inscription on the tomb of Phytalus:

The hero and king Phytalus here gave welcome to Demeter, the revered goddess, at the time when she was creating the first fruit of the harvest; men have given it the name of the sacred fig; whence Phytalus and his heirs derive immortal honour.

Plutarch tells how, in the time of Theseus, a holy symbol known as Eiresione would be created from an olive branch wrapped in wool and would be carried in procession to this prayer-chant:

> Eiresione bring figs, and Eiresione bring loaves;
> Bring us honey in pints, and oil to rub our bodies,
> And a strong flagon of wine, so that all go mellow to bed.

The chant presents a charmingly modest Mediterranean version of luxury and plenty. We notice, of course, that figs are named first, before even bread and wine, and we are struck by the simple delights of the Aegean paradise which Eiresione is requested to provide.

Also in Greek legend we find the story of the combat of the seers, recorded by Hesiod and others. Calchas challenges Mopsus to say how many figs are growing on one especially heavily laden tree. Mopsus gives his answer as 10,001. The figs are then carefully harvested and counted and are found to number . . . 10,001.

It appears that in earliest times figs may have been an exclusive food in mainland Greece, a food for the rich and for religious use, but that in later centuries they were more easily available and hence became a staple food of the poor. Plutarch believed the tradition that Solon forbade the export of figs, sometime around 590 BC, and that the law was vigorously enforced. Those who tried to smuggle figs out of Attica were liable to be reported to the authorities by 'those who reveal figs' (*sykophantes*), a fascinating etymology for 'sycophancy'.

The Athenian statesman Solon the Lawgiver (638–558 BC), who had strong views on figs.

The early importance of figs in Cyprus is manifested by the use of the same word *syke* in place names there. The name of the little village of Aglasyka means 'excellent figs' while the better-known village of Makrasyka, near Famagusta, which is Incirli in Turkish, means 'long figs' in both languages.

Several writers emphasize that although the Greeks defined themselves principally by the olive, the gift of Athena, they sometimes defined themselves also by the fig. References can be found contrasting the civilized fig-eating Greeks with the barbarous Medes 'who know neither wine nor figs'. In Book III of *The Deipnosophists* (third century AD), among many pages on the glories of Greek figs, Athenaeus quotes Herodotus as believing that the fig is the most useful to man of all the fruits which grow on trees. He also quotes a certain Magnus as saying,: 'the fig tree, my friends, is the guide to men to lead them to a more civilized life', and the comic writer Antiphanes writing that Attica was superior to all other lands in honey, bread and figs. Figs are portrayed here as a yardstick and a symbol of the highest levels of civilization.

Athenaeus' book is packed full of figgy anecdotes and quotation after quotation, often from authors now lost. He cites the story of Anchimolus and Moschus, as told by Hegesander: they were sophists living in Elis, and all their adult lives they drank only water and ate only figs; they were as healthy and vigorous as any other men, but their sweat smelt so offensive that everyone avoided them at the public baths. He believed that figs were especially good for children, and quotes Herodotus once again, making the intriguing suggestion that children fed on fig juice would grow to a great size. He also believed that figs were the most digestible of all fruit, which was proved by the fact that Greeks would eat far more figs than all other fruit put together. Then he gives us a Greek proverb in a format that appears in the food proverbs of many cultures: 'Figs after fish, vegetables after meat.'

Athenaeus was aware of the distinction between brebas and figs, and he cites Aristophanes, Theophrastus and other Greek authors to illustrate the fact that some types of fig trees, some years, will bear two crops.

Greek literature is constantly enriched by references to figs, mostly in terms of reverence or pleasure. Many of the references in Homer and Hesiod are to fig trees rather than fig fruit, although the reference in *The Odyssey* to the delights of the fruit trees which are seen to tantalize Tantalus during Odysseus' descent into the underworld refers to purple figs:

> Above, beneath, around his hapless head,
> Trees of all kinds spread their delicious fruit
> There figs, sky-tinted, showed their purple hue,
> Olives shone green, and pomegranates glowed.

Figs, olives and pomegranates: these were Homer's idea of the three fruits most likely to tantalize a Greek, although when Pindar retold the story in his poem known as 'Olympian 1', he had Tantalus tantalized by figs and pears.

Euripides (*c.* 480–406 BC) provides an insight into an interesting technique of food production when, in *The Cyclops*, one of the foods which Silenus offers to sell to Odysseus is cheese curdled with fig juice. According to modern-day cheese-makers, this is more likely to have been the white sap or latex from a fig branch than the juice from a fruit.

The poet Archilocus, writing around 700 BC, described the cultivation of figs on the island of Paros, in the Cyclades (where figs are still extensively grown). And in his *The Science of Good Husbandry; or, The Oeconomics of Xenophon*, Xenophon (*c.* 430–354 BC) underlines Socrates' great interest in the art of growing grapes, figs and olives. Advising Socrates, Ischomachus stressed that figs should ideally be harvested individually, fig by fig, day by day, as each fruit reached its consummate ripeness.

Aristophanes (*c.* 446–386 BC) was one of the Greek writers who referred most frequently to figs, usually in a spirit of hilarity as well as pleasure. In *The Acharnians*, he made fun of the young girls' greed for figs:

Soaring to the sun.

Hey, you're squealing boldly for the figs.
Bring out the figs then, one of you indoors,
For these girlie greedy pigs.
Will they eat them though, I wonder.
Worshipful Herakles! look at them gobbling now!

In *The Wasps*, the boy's special prayer turns out to be for dainty sweet figs, while in *Clouds* Strepsiades reflects on his marriage: his ladylike wife was always sweetly perfumed and smelling of saffron, while he himself, a simple country boy, goes to bed 'smelling fresh and fruity, like ripe figs and new wool'. In *Plutus*, Plutus himself says 'it does not become our poet to throw figs and sweetmeats among the spectators in order to

Aristophanes, who used figs in the humour of his plays.

bribe their applause'. And in *The Suits* Panaetis comes up with another original fig image: 'You devour the ministers of finance as though they were figs, squeezing them to see which is still green, which ripe, and which bursting out his seeds.'

Following the expiration of Solon's prohibition on the export of figs, we find numerous examples of Greek figs being sought by representatives of other civilizations, including those in India. In the third century BC, Bindusara, king of the Maurya lands in India, wrote to Greece requesting three things: some grape syrup, some figs and a philosopher. Grape syrup and figs, he was told politely, would be sent to him with pleasure, but it was against Greek law to trade in philosophers.

In the later years of Spartan dominance, frugal eating and communal living were imposed norms, especially under the rule of Lycurgus. The Spartans met, according to Plutarch, in groups of fifteen and each member of the company had to provide his monthly contribution of a bushel of meal, eight gallons of wine, five pounds of cheese, two and a half pounds of figs, and a small sum of money to buy meat or fish. Again we find figs numbered among the absolute necessities of Greek life, even in times of Spartan frugality.

The Phallic Fig

'Dr Aigremont', a pseudonymous author who in 1908 published a scholarly treatise in German on popular traditions of love and sex (*Volkserotik*), paid particular attention to the fig. He identified the fig as a symbol of fertility and propagation in many oriental countries, but above all in ancient Greece. Figs were sacred to Dionysus and the huge phallus carried at Dionysian festivals would be carved from fig wood – in memory of the fig-wood phallus which Dionysus was said to have placed on the grave of Polyhymnus. The fig was also sacred to the phallic godling Priapus, and priapic images would similarly be carved in fig wood. The sexual connotations of the fig were further evident in the obscene fig gesture, known to the Greeks and Romans, with the thumb pushed up between two fingers. Still current in Italy as *far la fica*, and present in Dante's *Inferno* as *Le mani alzò con amendue le fiche*, the fig gesture is further discussed in the final chapter. The aphrodisiac qualities of the fig were widely credited in early societies, and appear still to be so in modern Turkey, where, in the tourist areas of Istanbul at least, dried figs are prominently and ubiquitously advertised as 'Turkish Viagra'.

5
Figs in Ancient Rome

Like the Greeks, the Romans venerated figs and fig trees. They especially celebrated the first day of the year with figs. In Ovid's *Fasti* (AD 8), Janus explains that gifts of dates, dried figs and honey to propitiate the gods as the year opened were omens to ensure that the year would begin in sweetness in order that it could continue in sweetness. These practices, typical of the clumsy but attractive functionalism of Roman religion, were to prove remarkably durable. Gillian Riley, in her canonical *Oxford Companion to Italian Food* (2007), notes the Roman practices, specifying that the dates and figs would be preserved in the honey, and tells us that these ancient traditions are still honoured in the vicinity of Naples, where local people exchange figs which are wrapped in laurel leaves, and in Campania and Abruzzo, where the typical gift for the start of the year is dried figs stuffed with almonds.

Although figs grow perfectly well in Italy, they were thought to ripen even better in the warmer lands to the south and east. The ancient Romans imported figs, notably from North Africa, and Plutarch and others tell the story of how Cato the Elder deliberately dropped some 'Libyan' figs from his toga on to the floor of the Senate. When the senators admired the size and beauty of the figs, Cato

Figs on a fresco at Poppea's Villa, Oplontis, 50 BC.

enthusiastically agreed but then pointed out that they were from Carthage – only three days' voyage from Rome. This underlined his constant theme that Carthage must be destroyed.

Virgil does not mention figs in *The Georgics* (*c.* 29 BC), but this is no great loss given his notorious ignorance about trees and grafting. His contemporary Varro was better informed. Varro believed that fig culture was part of the earliest ways of life on Rome's Palatine Hill, and, like Pliny, saw a close association between figs and milk. Romulus's sacred fig tree was closely associated with Rumina the milk goddess (it was called interchangeably 'the ficus Ruminalis' and 'the ficus Romularis'). Three main reasons have been suggested for this association: confusion between the names; the compatibility of figs and milk as foodstuffs; and the visual similarity between milk and the milky sap which flows from fig wood. All three may contain some truth. In any event, figs, fig wood and the sacred fig tree were seen as defining elements in religious celebrations in ancient Rome.

Clodius Albinus (d. AD 197), an aristocratic consul, ruler of Britain and aspirant emperor, was a great advocate of the high-Roman diet comprising mostly vegetables and fruit (in contrast with the Barbarian diet, which was heavy in meat and milk products). It is reported that Clodius was a greedy fruit eater, capable of breaking his fast with 500 figs, a basket of peaches, ten melons and 20 lb of grapes. Many fig-lovers in a good number of countries have been consulted in the course of researching this book, and all of them have blanched at the idea of eating 500 figs at one sitting!

The Romans spread fig production into several of their colonies, especially the islands of the western Mediterranean. Local sources in both Corsica and Mallorca, for example, attribute the origins of their fig crops to Roman introduction, and to this day the Mallorcan farmers continue the Roman practice of feeding windfall and sun-dried figs to their pigs, in the certain belief that it gives the best of all flavours to their pork.

Many Roman writers wrote about figs, and in many different contexts. Marcus Aurelius wrote pleasantly about bread, figs and olives which are ripe and ready:

> For example when bread is baked some parts split open at the surface, and these split parts, although contrary to the baker's art, have their own beauty and attraction, and excite a wish to eat. In the same way, figs, when perfectly ripe, gape open, and in the case of ripe olives the very fact that they are close to rottenness brings a special beauty to the fruit.

The authors already cited refer to figs in an easy and familiar way. There are numerous references to figs in Ovid's works, usually to dried figs, sometimes to dried figs mixed with dried dates. Cato's treatise *On Agriculture* (*c.* 160 BC) is full of advice on how to produce the best-quality figs. Varro speaks of cakes made from figs and spelt, and (mysteriously, given that fig trees have no flowers) states and then repeats that honey which bees make from figs is insipid, compared, for example, to the excellent honey which bees derive from clover. This is the only historical reference I know of to bees making honey from figs.

Cicero tells a famous story about the importance of puns and omens in Roman political life. As Marcus Crassus was about to depart from Brindisi in 55 BC on a military expedition which would turn out to be a disaster, he was approached by a fig-seller who called out 'Cauneas' (figs from Caunea). Cicero says that Crassus should have read the punning omen in the fig-seller's cry (*Cave ne eas*, meaning 'Don't go'), and that if he had heeded the warning the whole history of Rome would have been different.

The most knowledgeable Roman writer on figs was Pliny the Elder, whose vast and encyclopaedic *Natural History*, written around AD 75, aspires to cover the worlds of nature, technology and culture. Pliny devotes several chapters to figs, and even has some partial knowledge of caprification – described in the famous translation by Bostock and Riley of 1855:

> The fig, the only one among all the pomes, hastens to maturity by the aid of a remarkable provision of Nature. The wild-fig, known by the name of 'caprificus', never ripens itself, though it is able to impart to the others the principle of which it is thus destitute; for we occasionally find Nature

Figs and bread, Roman fresco.

making a transfer of what are primary causes, and being
generated from decay. To effect this purpose the wild fig-
tree produces a kind of gnat. These insects, deprived of all
sustenance from their parent tree, at the moment that it is
hastening to rottenness and decay, wing their flight to
others of kindred though cultivated kind. There feeding
with avidity upon the fig, they penetrate it in numerous
places, and by thus making their way to the inside, open the
pores of the fruit. The moment they effect their entrance,
the heat of the sun finds admission too, and through the
inlets thus made the fecundating air is introduced.

Pliny's description of the fruit itself remains unsurpassed:

All figs are soft to the touch, and when ripe contain grains in the interior. The juice, when the fruit is ripening, has the taste of milk, and when dead ripe, that of honey. If left on the tree they will grow old; and when in that state, they distil a liquid that flows in tears like gum. Those that are more highly esteemed are kept for drying, and the most approved kinds are put away for keeping in baskets. The figs of the island of Ebusus are the best as well as the largest, and next to them are those of Marrucinum. Where figs are in great abundance, as in Asia, for instance, huge jars are filled with them, and at Ruspina, a city of Africa, we find casks used for a similar purpose: here, in a dry state, they are extensively used instead of bread, and indeed as a general article of provision.

There are two new ideas in this text by Pliny: first, his opinion that the much-contested title of 'best figs' belongs to those of the island of Ebusus (the modern Ibiza); and second, that the figs reserved by the Romans for drying and preserving were the highest-quality figs. This was certainly not true in

Rabbit and figs, a fresco which survived the eruption of Vesuvius at Herculaneum in AD 79.

other ancient cultures. Ruspina, where figs were so abundant that they were kept in large casks and extensively used instead of bread, is the present-day holiday resort of Monastir in Tunisia, not far from the ruins of Carthage (the Phoenician Qart-Hadasht).

The best-known Roman food writer, Apicius, may have been a real person living in the reign of Tiberius but was more likely a convenient title for a later anthology. He was an early advocate of the careful matching of tastes (the essence of gastronomy), and one of his recommendations was for figs as an accompaniment to boiled or baked ham (as in 'Ham boiled with figs and bay leaves, then rubbed with honey'). He also recommended feeding figs to geese and pigs in order to improve the flavour of their meat. He was an admirer of fig wine, both for drinking and for cooking; for example, he suggested that chicken could be boiled in fig wine flavoured with dill seeds, dried mint, mustard and vinegar.

The works of the satirist Juvenal use fig imagery repeatedly. His bitter description of a parvenu who now 'sits above him', in *Satire III*, depicts someone who not so long ago was sailing to Rome below decks among all the rotten figs (from Naples or Sicily perhaps). In another satire he refers to a Roman version of *foie gras*, with the geese being force-fed a paste made from figs, water, wine and honey until their livers swelled to a great size. The pâté flavoured with figs, wine and honey was considered a great delicacy, and in ancient Rome – as in France to this day – might then be eaten accompanied by fresh figs.

A refinement on this, as the Roman Empire moved towards its decadent period, was the report by Columella (*c.* AD 4–70) of a recipe for baked thrushes which had been fed on dried figs pre-chewed by slaves.

In a similar spirit of decadence, Petronius Arbiter (*c.* AD 27–66) used fig imagery to illustrate a rather different subject in *The Satyricon*'s advice to wives whose husbands favour sodomy. The advice was to turn a blind eye to the husband's young boyfriends rather than to try to service the preference themselves:

> They give what a wife will not give. 'I grant that favour', you say, 'rather than that my husband's love should wander from my bed'. It is not the same thing. I want the fig of Chios, not a flavourless fig; and in you this Chian fig is flavourless. A woman of sense and a wife ought to know her place.

Despite the dubious context and the unpleasant tone, it is interesting to note that the figs of Chios are used as a symbol for supreme pleasure. (Modern guidebooks still state that Chios is famous for mastic, olives and figs.)

Finally, moving from anal sex to murder, two famous deaths in the Roman era are closely associated with figs. According to the best-known story, Cleopatra decided that she had to die after Mark Antony's death, and chose to poison herself with the bite of an asp. The asp was conveyed to her in a basket of figs. The later death of Cleopatra's former antagonist Augustus (previously Octavian) is more uncertain. The authors Dio Cassius and Tacitus give credence to the rumour that his wife Livia took advantage of his notorious love of figs in order to poison him. Dio Cassius portrays Livia painting poison on to the finest figs still growing on Augustus' own trees. The rumours around Augustus' unexplained death may even have been stirred by the role of figs in the death of Cleopatra. Pliny the Elder suggests a different connection, telling us that Livia herself was a great expert on figs and brought a new variety to Rome, which became known as Livian figs.

6

The Crusaders and Figs
in Medieval Europe

The Mediterranean fig-growing area extended during the medieval period. In particular, the Moorish conquests in the Iberian peninsula brought fig production on a large scale to Spain and Portugal, which proved to be climatically very well suited and where figs quickly became a crucial part of the Iberian diet. The household accounts of Henry VIII, as we shall see, pay particular attention to a gift of a basket of Portuguese figs received by the king.

With this spread into Spain and Portugal, the entire Mediterranean region became a fig-growing zone. As such, by late medieval times, the zone of the olive (used by the social historian Fernand Braudel as a key definition of 'Mediterranean') was very closely matched by the zone of the fig – the difference being that figs continued to grow extensively in the lands of their origin in Arabia and Mesopotamia.

Throughout southern Europe figs were revered and given the highest possible food status, in spite of their abundance in their season (especially the early autumn). They also began to be more widely known and, as fresh figs, even more highly valued in the countries of northern Europe in which, certainly until around the year 1100, fig trees hardly grew at all.

Crusaders marching in a stained-glass window from Brussels Cathedral.

It seems probable that a crucial factor in the spread of a love of figs through northern Europe was the encounter with figs, from the year 1095 onwards, by the invading Crusaders. The northern knights brought back many new food preferences from their barbarous Levantine adventures, and one of them was figs.

The Crusaders, known to the Arabs as al-Franj, encountered new sights, new smells and new tastes, as well as new temperatures, as they travelled south from Constantinople. Everything seemed strange and exotic in the heat hazes as they passed through Turkey and Syria. In the earliest years of the invasions, the response to the exotic sights and places tended to be hatred and savage brutality, as evidenced in the massacres of Jerusalem (1099) and Beirut (1110), and barbarian savagery continued to be typical of some later invaders, most notably King Richard 1 of England. But in a good number of cases, the Franj warriors started to show signs of going native, forming local alliances, and regarding some of the towns, such as Antioch and Sidon, as their oriental homes. The lush fruit and the Levantine orchards warrant frequent mention in the Crusader accounts of the lands they were occupying. For many of the Franj settlers, the victories of Saladin (Salāh al-Dīn) between 1187 and 1192 seemed like an eviction from paradise.

The littoral area remained longer in Western hands, and the lands around Tyre and Acre in particular were occupied by Venetian settlers, following the successes of the fleet of Doge Domenico Michiel (d. 1130). The Venetians acquired orchards of lemons, oranges, almonds and figs. The Venetian fig-growers around Tyre were especially known and admired; but such ownerships were only for a fortunate few. Most Crusaders had to return north with their memories.

Various personal accounts and chronicles tell how the flavours and perfumes of the Near East entranced the Crusaders. The lemons, orange water, rose water and tamarind from these lands captivated their palates. Some strange legacies have been left by the encounter with such tastes – none stranger than 'brown sauce' (perhaps best known under the brand name HP Sauce). Now a commonplace accompaniment to the full English breakfast, it was originally an intriguing mix of tamarinds, oriental fruits and spices, sugars and vinegars which the Crusaders found new and wonderful.

The attention of the Crusaders was captured both by new combinations and wholly new flavours. Some were crude and strong, such as the mixtures which we now find in brown sauce and Christmas pudding; some were unthought-of food pairings, like sweet mint sauce with lamb; others were light

Picking figs, from the 14th-century illuminated manuscript *Tacuinum Sanitatis*.

and exquisite, such as rose water and fresh figs. The Crusaders coveted all these exotic flavours, crude or subtle, and wished to transport them northwards. They sought to create import–export routes, and these worked well for spices, almonds, dates and candied fruits. They were no use, however, for the highly perishable and seasonal fresh figs. As a result, some of the more optimistic returning Franj began to look at ways of transporting fig trees to the north – trying to protect them from the northern winters and to maximize their exposure to the paler summer sun.

Fig trees were thus introduced into sheltered south-facing corners of gardens in northern Europe. The example most often cited is the Disiboden cloister garden in Germany, where the figs and other exotics have been convincingly attributed to Crusader influence. Religious cloisters came to have a particular association with fig trees. Even in England, a fig tree in Lambeth Palace is said to have been planted by Cardinal Pole around the 1520s, and a fig tree on the estate of Archbishop Cranmer is said to have been

Figs decorating a Levantine plate.

imported from Italy and planted by the archbishop himself, probably in the 1530s.

There is one remarkable English source, from as early as 1257. That was a year of extremely severe weather, and Matthew Paris, a Benedictine monk based at St Albans Abbey, reported that 'the fig trees were almost all destroyed.' The evocative phrase and especially the words 'almost all' imply that there was a good number of destroyed fig trees and, this being our earliest English source, we are left to wonder whether perhaps their recent planting was a contributory factor in their destruction, and whether this is an early reference to a Crusader introduction.

We do have one English reference which is even earlier, although there is no written evidence. There has long been a strong local tradition that a 'White Marseilles' fig tree growing in the Tarring Fig Gardens near Worthing was a descendant of a tree first planted there by Thomas à Becket around 1162, the year he became archbishop of Canterbury. Becket was closely associated with the Crusades, and his murderers were sent to do penance by crusading in Palestine, where some of them are said to be buried in Jerusalem.

Throughout this period (from the twelfth century to the fifteenth), the big cities were fig cities. There was no European city of the population of either Istanbul or Cairo. These were the two great centres of the Western and Near Eastern world, and in addition Aleppo, Damascus and Tunis were city states and market centres of similar size and significance to Venice, Florence and Paris. The market structure of the world which had the Mediterranean Sea as its centre was therefore perfectly adapted for the export and import of figs, especially dried figs. The problems which intervened were of wars and alliances, trade routes and transport methods. The position in respect of these problems was very slow to improve. As early

Seller of dried figs, from the 14th-century illuminated manuscript *Tacuinum Sanitatis*.

as the 1180s, Saladin, that most enlightened of rulers, had courted controversy by setting up trading arrangements with the Venetians and other Christian city states. The Church in the West and Islamic hardliners in Saladin's own lands were outraged by this trade, and for many centuries religious bigotry was as big a problem for the fig trade as transportation.

The Myth which Seduced the Crusaders

The Crusader and chronicler Jean de Joinville, writing around 1305, produced a much-respected life of the French king Louis IX, but the biography also included an account of how the fishermen of the River Nile cast their nets and hauled in exotic products such as ginger, rhubarb, aloes and cinnamon, 'and it is said that these goods flow from the earthly paradise'. No one can be sure whether Joinville truly believed that the Garden of Eden lay up-Nile and allowed its products to be borne northwards by the great river, but this sort of semi-mythological account of the mysterious and exotic Orient was common between the twelfth and fourteenth centuries. Those wondrous distant lands, conceived, in the words of the French historian Jacques Le Goff, as *un horizon onirique* (a horizon of dreams), were laden with images of paradise, especially in respect of their foods.

The Crusaders were seduced by this myth. Some of them sought to gain ownership of the Palestinian land around Acre and Tyre, with its orchards of lemons, oranges, almonds and figs. But most had to try to find ways to bring that exotic distant paradise of dreams home with them, back to northern Europe.

7
All Around the World: The Modern History

Figs remained rare in the north, however. Although they were planted in some palaces and cloisters, often their fruit did not ripen properly. Figs are not mentioned at all in the general works of Thomas Tusser and Francis Bacon, and several of their contemporaries commented upon the difficulty of getting figs to ripen in England.

Henry Phillips, in his excellent book *The Companion for the Orchard* (1831), doubted the ability of figs to thrive in England in the past or the present, except in protected walled corners or in botanical gardens, where extraordinary results could sometimes be achieved:

> At the Royal Gardens at Kew, there was a fig-house fifty feet in length, where, under the superintendence of Mr Aiton, this fruit has been forced to the highest pitch of perfection: Mr Aiton's chief reliance has been, we understand on the second crop. In the year 1810, the royal tables were supplied with more than two hundred baskets of figs from that fig-house, fifty baskets of which were from the first crop, and one hundred and fifty baskets from the second. In one instance, Mr Aiton had this fruit ripe in January, and sent excellent figs to

the palace on the late Queen Charlotte's birth-day, the 18th of that month.

For Britain, northern France and all of northern Europe, transportation was the key to access to figs. For as long as transport was difficult, they remained a rare and luxurious product. When transport improved, or when a military alliance was formed with a fig-producing country, access became easier.

In southern Europe, figs were grown extensively in most Mediterranean countries at the time of the fall of the Roman Empire. The fig-growing zone was then extended by the Moorish conquests, into Spain and Portugal and across North Africa. Fig production in Spain and Portugal came to be even more important than in Italy and Greece. Figs grew well in southern France, and Thomas Jefferson, visiting Marseilles and Toulon in 1787, suggested that the French figs were the most delicately flavoured of all.

Figs on a stall in Croatia.

Figs went from Spain to the Americas, and it is claimed that the oldest fig tree in the New World is the Pizarro tree in the governor's palace in Lima, probably planted around 1540. Figs were introduced to Mexico by Hernán Cortés, perhaps in the 1530s, and it was soon discovered that Mexico and California provided good climates for fig production.

The Spanish also took fig trees to their new colonies in the Canary Islands, from the fifteenth century, only to find that figs were already there. The archaeologist Jacob Morales, of the Universidad de Las Palmas de Gran Canaria, reports that figs were certainly introduced into Gran Canaria and Tenerife in the pre-Hispanic period, with archaeological evidence dating back to the sixth century AD. Morales reports archaeological findings of fig seeds not only around excavated human sites but also (as the ultimate proof) within the cavities of human teeth. Of the seafaring nations which are known or believed to have visited the Canary Islands (and perhaps originated the myth of a heavenly Atlantis there), this date would be too late for the Phoenicians and too early for the Normans. It would perhaps make the most likely introducers of figs into 'the fortunate isles' either the Carthaginians or the Romans.

Figs were seen in England in the Middle Ages as an exotic Mediterranean fruit. For Shakespeare the fruit was 'the fig of Spain' (*Henry V*, III.vi). He also associated figs with Egypt, having Charmian say 'I love long life better than figs' (*Antony and Cleopatra*, I.ii). Connections were made at this time with figs from Palestine through the story that Jesus Christ desired to eat figs along the road to Bethany, leading to the medieval English tradition of eating figgy pudding on a Lenten Sunday.

Looking at English archival sources, port records show that figs (presumably dried) were being extensively imported into England by the mid-fourteenth century and then through

The multi-trunked fig tree at the Picasso Museum in Malaga.

the fifteenth century. Ports such as Sandwich and Exeter (both much more important in medieval times than now) record cargoes of figs, especially from Italy. A more exclusive archival source, the privy purse accounts of Henry VIII, records a gift to the king from a Mr Worsley of Portuguese figs. It is probable that these would have been fresh figs – truly a dainty dish to set before a king.

Post-medieval European society adopted the fig into the role which it had filled in the ancient societies of the Greeks and the Romans. The fig became the fruit of festivities, and especially of autumn and winter festivities, in northern Europe as well as the Mediterranean region.

In England, figs became the typical fruit of the post-Dickensian family Christmas. Along with Christmas trees, Christmas stockings, Santa Claus, tinsel and images of robins in snow-covered gardens, dried figs were an essential component. Indeed, in many English families in the nineteenth and twentieth centuries, dried figs were eaten only on Christmas Day and the days following. A contemporary of Dickens tells us that in the 1830s the best dried figs in England were held to come from Turkey, Italy, Spain and Provence, in that order.

Long before Dickens, figgy pudding was established as an English Christmas treat. In some homes it may still be. As Christmas 2008 approached, the *Daily Telegraph*, that bastion of traditional Englishness, ran an article (12 December 2008) headed 'Figgy Pudding's Welcome Christmas Return', telling us:

> From the 16th century, figgy pudding traditionally appeared at the end of a Christmas meal – it is on the table of Bob Cratchit in *A Christmas Carol* – though it used to be served on Palm Sunday.

The most famous commemoration of figgy pudding at Christmas is surely from the well-known song 'We Wish You a Merry Christmas', which appears to be a secular hymn dating to the sixteenth century. This is its most Christmassy refrain:

> Oh, bring us a figgy pudding
> Oh, bring us a figgy pudding
> Oh, bring us a figgy pudding
> And a cup of good cheer.

It is not certain that the *Daily Telegraph* was wholly correct about Palm Sunday, but the assertion was not far from the truth. Fig Sunday (also known as Figpie Wake) is certainly mentioned in sources on folklore and custom as falling on a Sunday in Lent. Some sources specify the Sunday before Easter; others imply an earlier Sunday in Lent, with a link to the strange story of Jesus Christ and the fruitless fig tree on the road to Bethany.

There is no known explanation as to why the traditional figgy pudding or fig pie should have become associated with Christmas rather than Lent. Its connection with a Lenten Sunday was perhaps rather tenuous, deriving from the story of Jesus cursing a fig tree for not being in fruit at a time of year when no fig tree, outside of a botanical garden, would be in fruit; one might rather have expected it to be celebrated for its autumnal ripeness, as in a harvest festival. Celebrations of curses are rare. The switching of the figgy pudding's allegiance to Christmas makes practical and seasonal sense, and possibly this came to override the original scriptural connection.

The Story of Fig Wasps in California

The year 1769 is usually given as the date for the first planting of fig trees in California. It was then that Franciscan missionaries led by Padre Junípero Serra established the Mission at San Diego and transplanted fruit trees from Baja California. Subsequently, the same type of Spanish-Mexican fig was planted at missions along the southern Californian coast, and it came to be known by the variety name Black Mission. In 1798 Jean-François de Galaup la Pérouse made a list of the fruit trees brought on shipboard from France bound for California, which included three white figs, two Angélique and two violet species. Fig trees were recorded by George Vancouver in the mission garden at Santa Clara in 1792 and at Ventura in 1793. The gardens at the San Gabriel Mission thirty years later included many fig trees. The Black Mission and other varieties which arrived early in California were among the types of fig which do not require pollination in order to fruit. The thriving of Black Mission figs (an 'Adriatic' variety), in particular in the vicinities of San Diego and Santa Clara, led the Californian growers into false expectations as other varieties of fig – the great European and Turkish varieties – began to be imported.

In the later nineteenth century, many fine fig trees (especially of the Smyrna type) failed to produce viable fruit in California, to the consternation of their importers. The figs were falling from the trees before they had ripened and the fig-growers, expecting Turkish-style quantities of ripe fruit, were in despair. The 1880s was a terrible decade for Californian figs, and there were strong suspicions that the Turks, jealous of their lucrative export market, were deliberately sending sterile fig trees to California.

The true explanation was different, and was already known to some fig experts, but there was a profound reluctance to accept it. The explanation was that many types of fig tree, including the excellent Turkish varieties exported to California in the 1880s, require the pollinating intervention of fig wasps. But there was strong resistance to Turkish peasant lore and practices (including the manual insertion of fig wasps into the fruit), which was seen as backward superstition, and also to the import of Turkish insects into the USA.

The 1890s were a time of great debate about the role of fig wasps. Learned papers were published on the role of the little insects, with their rather wonderful scientific name of blastophaga, and on the art of 'caprification' (pollinating and ripening figs by the introduction of fig wasps). The progression towards fully ripened Californian figs was seriously impeded by the publication in 1892 of an influential article by the late Italian fig expert Guglielmo Gasparrini (d. 1866), in which Turkish peasant practices were denounced: 'Caprification is useless for the setting and ripening of the fruit and this custom, which entails expense and deteriorates the flavour of the fig, ought to be abolished from our agriculture.'

Only with time and detailed study did horticulturalists come to understand that Italian figs and Turkish figs might ripen in different ways. Greek figs tend to resemble the Turkish varieties, and the fact that Greek authors of the eminence of Aristotle and Theophrastus had been describing caprification since the fourth century BC leaves little excuse for the Californian experts who at first decided to follow the advice of Professor Gasparrini.

It was only around 1900 that the advocates of caprification in California won the argument, after two decades of debate. Californian horticulturalists were well aware that within any genus of fruit there can be species which require pollinating and species which do not, because the different orange crops already prospering in California had exactly those different requirements (the Washington navel orange growing near Fresno needed no pollination, whereas the more widespread Valencia late oranges did). For some reason, however, the fig-growers resisted applying the same thinking to their crops. As a result, the Lob Injir and other Smyrna figs failed to set fruit and produced no viable figs until caprification began (on a small scale during the 1890s and commercially after 1900).

The first major shipment of fig wasps arrived in the U.S. in March 1898, and by a pleasing irony they came from southern Italy, near Naples. The Italian wasps, however, failed to pollinate successfully, probably because they arrived too late in the year. The next year a consignment of Algerian fig wasps arrived – following a special visit by officials of the Department of Agriculture to the Jardin Botanique in Algiers and more successful pollination began. The wasps were transported from Algeria inside caprifigs, and fortunately the

Californian climate was to their liking. In the winter of 1899–1900 it was reported that many thousands of Algerian blastophaga were happily overwintering in California and were buzzing around the Lob Injir trees. A further importation of Greek fig wasps in 1899 by W. T. Swingle, a specially appointed 'agricultural explorer' of the Department of Agriculture, was similarly successful. By 1901 caprified figs were beginning to be produced in California in large quantities; by 1908 Mr Swingle was able to publish a learned work on the triumph of caprification; and by the 1920s thousands of tons of caprified figs were being produced each year in California. As late as 1898 Swingle had been publicly ridiculed when he presented his ideas on caprification to an Italian audience; the success was no doubt especially sweet for him. Caprification became, from about 1900, the new orthodoxy. The reputation of both the fig wasp and the Turkish peasant fig farmer had been redeemed.

Following the success of Californian caprification, a number of suitable climates in the southern hemisphere were identified and fig production was commercially introduced in South Africa, Australia, Argentina and Chile. The 'fig capital of South Africa' is Klein Karoo in the Western Cape, where tourists can book rooms for a holiday of fig gluttony on one of the local fruit farms. The extraordinary multi-trunked Wonderboom fig tree, however (which is supposedly the most famous tree in Africa), is not a cultivated fruit tree but a wild willowleaf fig.

The fig industry in California was successful but comparatively minor until the late 1960s, when the aftermath of the Arab–Israeli War of 1967 dramatically reduced the supply of figs from their homelands to the u.s. and the West. Fig plantation in California more than doubled between 1968 and 1971.

The fig wasp at work, burrowing into the top of a fig.

With improvements to horticultural practices and with cross-breeding and the creation of new and hardier species, there has been a considerable expansion of the lands where fig trees are able to prosper. It is even possible now to eat outdoor-grown English figs – a superbly fruiting 'Brown Turkey' tree grows happily, for example, in the garden of Cliff Cottage, Lyme Regis, overlooking The Cobb. In *The Gourmet Gardener* (2005), Bob Flowerdew recommends species such as Brown Turkey and also 'Brunswick', grown from cuttings, not seed, and fertilized with seaweed and potash, not with nitrogen. Flowerdew notes the tradition of confining the roots within a wooden box frame, but takes the view that this is unnecessary provided that heavy feeding is avoided. Although outdoor fruiting is entirely possible, especially in sheltered and seaside locations, growth under glass is still recommended for the English climate if the fruit are to ripen perfectly. Hugh Fearnley-Whittingstall notes the preponderance in England of the hardy 'Brown Turkey', but (for growing under glass)

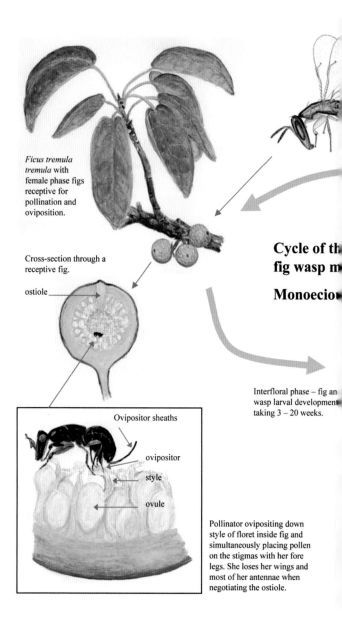

Ficus tremula tremula with female phase figs receptive for pollination and oviposition.

Cross-section through a receptive fig.

ostiole

Cycle of th
fig wasp m

Monoecio

Interfloral phase – fig an
wasp larval development
taking 3 – 20 weeks.

Ovipositor sheaths

ovipositor

style

ovule

Pollinator ovipositing down style of floret inside fig and simultaneously placing pollen on the stigmas with her fore legs. She loses her wings and most of her antennae when negotiating the ostiole.

caenus clairae – a galling non-
ating fig wasp that enters the fig
iposition at the same time as the
ator.

Pollinator female *Courtella wardi*. On
leaving the natal fig she homes in on
volatiles released by receptive figs on
other trees.

Male phase figs, which will
ripen after release of wasps
and become attractive to
frugivores for seed dispersal.

Pollinator male *Courtella wardi*. After
mating with females, males chew an
exit hole through the fig wall, allowing
pollen laden females to escape from the
fig cavity.

Otitesella (right) and *Sycoryctes* (above) –
two non-pollinating fig wasps that
oviposit through the fig wall during the
interfloral phase. *Otitesella* species are
gall formers and *Sycoryctes* species are
parasitoids of galling fig wasps.

Illustration © Simon van Noort
(Iziko Museums of Cape Town)

The extraordinary life-cycle of figs and the fig wasp is outlined in this
diagram, created in the Iziko Museum in Cape Town.

recommends the better flavour of 'Rouge de Bordeaux', 'White Marseilles', 'Excel' or 'Petite Nigra'.

Fresh and Dried

Figs are best eaten fresh, and best of all freshly picked from the tree, but this inevitably limits their availability. Harold McGee, who knows more than anyone else about the chemistry of food flavours and tastes, tells us that when perfectly ripe figs have a unique aroma, this comes mainly from spicy phenolic compounds and a flowery terpene (linalool). The aroma is part of the uniquely delicious flavour of tree-ripened fresh figs.

No fruit is more perishable than the fig, however; only a day too late and it can become a soft squashy mess – although

Ripe and alluring in a basket.

Jammy figs.

the flavour and the nutritional value are unimpaired by the squashiness, and burst figs taste like the finest jam on earth.

From the earliest times, therefore, humans learned to preserve figs by drying them. Most dried figs are pressed flat before drying, but smaller luxury varieties may be dried upright, preserving their original shape. Outdoor sun-drying gives by far the best results, provided that the figs are regularly turned.

In early civilizations figs were often left to be sun-dried on the tree. This practice is still allowed to happen in some fig groves in North Africa, but in most of the major fig-producing countries sun-drying on wooden trays has long been the norm.

Figgy jams.

The best dried figs keep their shape.

The temptation to pick the fruit before it is fully ripe must be resisted, warn most of the fruit-farming manuals.

As fig-drying processes became less artisanal and more industrial, practices such as sulphuring became more common. The manuals recommend dipping in water and then sulphuring for about four hours before drying in the sun for between two and four days. Sulphuring is sometimes presented as a logical development of previous peasant or artisanal practices. In Portugal, for example, before drying, figs used to be thoroughly washed in water and then dipped in a mixture of brine and olive oil.

Dried figs are a nutritional product of excellent quality and have even become a staple food, helping poorer people to stay

Dried figs are a delicious staple food. When bread was in short supply, dried figs sustained the marching armies of Alexander the Great.

alive through the winters; but in the great majority of cases the exotic magic of the fig is lost somewhere in the drying process.

By the twentieth century the commercial value of figs extended far beyond their role as a food in their own right. Fig essence came to be widely used as a coffee substitute. Fig-flavoured and fig-filled biscuits became popular, beginning with Fig Newtons in the 1890s. Candied figs became a popular way of preserving and presenting firm fresh green figs, especially in America. Figs came to play a major role first in patent medicines (some of which were no more than quackery) and then in the commercial pharmaceutical trade. They were found, because of their high alkalinity, to be useful to those trying to give up smoking, while their 'demulcent' properties led to their inclusion as an ingredient in cough mixtures. They were prescribed for people with skin-pigmentation diseases. Above all, however, they were known as an excellent source of dietary fibre, with celebrated laxative qualities.

The Story of Syrup of Figs

The medicinal value of figs has been a constant theme in Middle Eastern, Levantine and Mediterranean societies, ever since its first mention, in Iraq, by King Urukagina, almost 5,000 years ago. The Greeks and Romans, in particular, believed that a healthy, largely vegetarian diet, strongly featuring figs, olives, grapes, bread and wine, was the key to their superiority over the meat-tearing, milky-smelling Barbarians.

More recently, a strong, and undoubtedly exaggerated, emphasis on the laxative qualities of figs has developed. It is probably this association above all which makes the story of Clodius Albinus and his 500 figs for breakfast so striking to the modern reader.

As the European and North American diets became more and more Barbarian in their emphasis on meat, dairy products and protein in general, the fig was asked to play a less glamorous role in helping the human body to assimilate the huge quantities of protein in the modern diet. For post-war northern European consumers, in particular, the association between figs and laxative action is often, very sadly, primary, and this is epitomized by a hideous concoction known as syrup of figs.

The use of fig juice as a mild and gentle laxative has been known from ancient times, and the general reverence for figs led to its having a benign reputation. In the great era of bad diet and patent medicine in the U.S. and northern Europe, however – roughly 1840–1940 – this reputation was adopted and abused by a far stronger laxative which was given the deceptively alluring name of syrup of figs. Syrup of figs did great harm to the reputation of our fruit of paradise, even though it was widely known that its principal active ingredient was not fig juice but senna, and even though several commercial brands of syrup of figs contained no figs at all, relying on a mixture of senna and rhubarb for their efficacy. The widespread use of syrup of figs, together with cold showers and caning, in British public schools was sometimes intended as punishment and sometimes thought to be character-building. As a result, in some quite elevated circles of British society, the dubious reputation of figs endures to this day.

The entertaining claims of the purveyors of patent medicines, especially in the period just before the First World War, can be enjoyed in medical museums such as the Wellcome Collection in London. Syrup of figs was recommended to give a bonny complexion, as well as to deal with weak, sluggish bowels and torpid livers.

Unlike some other famous patent medicines, such as Dr Williams' Pink Pills for Pale People or Dr MacKenzie's Improved Harmless Arsenic Complexion Wafers, syrup of figs has somehow managed to retain a measure of reputation and continues to be commercially available.

It may be permissible to add that, having purchased a bottle of syrup of figs from the UK's leading high-street chemists in order to assist with the writing of this section (active ingredients: 0.40 ml senna; 0.50 ml fig liquid extract), the author later took the precaution of emptying the contents down the sink.

Festive Figs in their Homelands

The modern history of the fig in southern Europe and the Near East is uncontaminated by such foul associations. In these homelands 'the time of the fig', the end of the harvest and the gathering together of the crop, has been and remains a time of pride and joy.

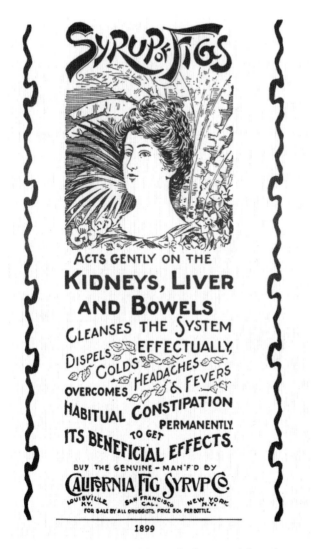

An advertisement for syrup of figs. In the first part of the 20th century, this dubious concoction was widely recommended for internal cleansing.

We noted the drunken ecstasy with which the fig crop is welcomed in Kabylie. The style of the Kabyle celebration may be unique, but in most of the fig-growing lands the bringing in of the fig crop will be accompanied by vibrant and vivid festivals and outpourings of joy. In France there are excellent examples in Solliès-Pont in Provence and Nézignan l'Evêque in Languedoc, among many others. So closely associated with figs are the inhabitants of Nézignan that they are known in the local language as *bécos figos* (fig-eaters, cognate with the French *becfigues* – birds known in English as fig-peckers). Solliès-Pont goes further and calls itself 'la capitale de la figue'. It is home to a proud and wonderful organization calling itself Le Syndicat de Défense de la Figue de Solliès (Union for the Protection of the Solliès Fig), which has self-confidently adopted the web address www.figue.org.

In the town of Peri, in southern Corsica, another exuberant fig festival (*festa di u ficu* in the Corsican language) is held in mid-September. This has become an international festivity, attracting fig-producers from Morocco, Tuscany and Provence, and its full story can be read at www.festadiuficu.com.

In the neighbourhood of Montuïri, in the plain of central Mallorca, the end of the fig harvest has long been extravagantly celebrated, usually in combination with a local saint's day, with all-night dancing and singing, and with ample quantities of the powerful local *licor de hierbas*, or *herbes* (alcohol flavoured with herbs), to strengthen the voices as the night would wear on. (There is a similar event in Peru, el Festival del Higo in the fig town of Chilca, but it is lubricated with pomegranate liqueur and, being in the southern hemisphere, takes place in February.)

The spectacular fig festivals of late summer in Poyales del Hoyo (in Ávila province in central Spain) and in Budva in Montenegro have gathered a growing fame, while in Turkey at the same period fig festivals abound, notably those of

Bursa, Aydin, Bilecik (which is a festival of figs and pome-granates, the combination noticed earlier in biblical, Arabic and Greek sources, as well as in Peru) and above all Izmir, which gave its previous name of Smyrna to one of the most famous of all types of fig.

The Near East Today

The major fig-producing countries of today's Near East – Egypt, Iran, Syria, Iraq, Israel, Yemen – are often in the news, but seldom or never in the context of fruit production. All these countries have a keen sense of continuity between the great civilizations of the past and life and culture in the present. One cannot understand the present aspirations of Iranians without some knowledge of the all-conquering and modernizing Iranian civilization of Cyrus the Great (known as 'the king of the world', d. *c.* 530 BC). In its small way, the cultural history of figs has to be part of this wider historical perspective.

To this day, figs remain an important cash-crop in their countries of origin – the modern states of both Yemen and Iraq. Production figures are not always dependable, but a league table of total fig production since 2000 would look something like this, for the leading countries:

1 Turkey	8 Syria	15 Libya
2 Egypt	9 USA	16 Portugal
3 Iran	10 Italy	17 Israel
4 Morocco	11 Mexico	18 Yemen
5 Algeria	12 Tunisia	19 Malta
6 Spain	13 Lebanon	
7 Greece	14 Iraq	

Clearly, if political conditions were to improve in Yemen and Iraq in the coming decades, there is scope and capacity for them both to move up this table.

Yemeni fig-growers have been proud to claim that the productivity of their fig groves has increased markedly, from 55,045 hectograms/hectares in 1979 to 107,697 hectograms/hectares in 2009. In Iraq, despite a considerable drop in annual fig production in 2003, fig farmers have thereafter managed to increase production once more in succeeding years, although the total crop in 2009 was still only around 80 per cent that of 2001, according to the Food and Agriculture Organization of the United Nations (FAO).

8

'Not Worth a Fig' or the Fruit of Heaven?

There is a fine story collected by the Victorian travel writer W.J.A. Stamer concerning a small sweet black fig called *mori* which, Stamer says, grows super-abundantly in the valleys of Cava de' Tirreni, in the historic kingdom of Naples. Many centuries ago the monks of Cava, needing a papal indulgence, decided to send two of their number to Rome to seek a concession from the pope. The envoys decided that they should take a gift of local produce to please the Holy Father, and, after considering and rejecting bunches of grapes and boxes of watermelons, they decided to take a gift of baskets of *mori*, those exquisitely delicious little figs which grew all around Cava. And so the envoys journeyed all the way to Rome and, ushered into the papal presence, offered their fig gift. His Holiness was enchanted by their present, and as the petition for the indulgence was carefully presented to him, he munched his way through fig after fig – and the envoys could see him appearing more and more benign as the sweetness of their fruit pervaded him. Before passing judgement on the request for an indulgence, His Holiness enquired as to where the delightful little fruit came from and how easily they could be found. Eager to please, and interrupting each other in their eagerness, the envoys told the pope that the figs were called

It's a balance.

mori; they were found everywhere in the vicinity of Cava; and, although they were so luxurious, they grew so copiously in the local valleys that peasants were able to feed them to their pigs. Rising up in indignation, the pope accused the envoys of bringing him their local pig food. Summoning the chief torturer of the Inquisition, the pope ordered that the two men should be placed in the stocks and pelted with their own figs until not one fruit remained. As they sat in the stocks, dripping with ripe fig pith, one envoy said to the other: 'Thank goodness we did not choose the watermelons, brother, for we would have been battered to death by now.'

The story illustrates the dichotomy in the way that figs can be at the same time, and even in the same place, both the most luxurious and valued of all fruits and the most copious and commonplace. Throughout literature and folklore there is this curious ambivalence about the value and status of the fig.

On the one hand, it is a luxury product, the supreme fruit and the king of the trees, with a long history of religious and celebratory significance, and a prized festive fruit. On the other hand, it has become a byword for a food which is so common as to be almost valueless – 'not worth a fig'.

Figs are one of a rare group of foods which belong on both sides of the great divide between the food of the rich and the food of the poor. In other writings, I have discussed the ways in which both salt cod (*bacalao*) and cheese can straddle that divide. To some extent, these special foods will do this by appearing in two forms: hard, long-duration cheese for the poor; soft and very perishable cheese for the rich; rock-hard, dried and salted yellow *bacalao* for the poor; white cod which has been salted but not dried for the rich (this became a regular feature of the banquets of Versailles, known as *morue verte*). In the same way, exquisite fresh figs are the luxury product, while dried figs can be a food staple to see the poor through the winter. We have to bear in mind, however, as the story from Cava de' Tirreni illustrates, that in their season and in their homelands the luscious and luxurious fresh figs are so universally available that they can feed pigs and popes alike.

Royal and seigneurial texts are good sources of information about the food of the rich, while recipe and culinary

Francisco Barrera, *Autumn*, 1638, oil on canvas, showing the fresh figs which grace autumn tables.

Francisco Barrera, *Winter*, 1638, oil on canvas, showing how preserved figs take their place on great tables during the cold season.

advice books also began to appear from the fourteenth century onwards. The earliest recipe books were written for professional cooks, who would have worked for the very rich, and typically include advice about avoiding over-hot foods which might burn the sensitive tongues of the mistresses and masters. Estate books, account books and household documents make possible the quantitative assessment of the food reaching the tables of the wealthy; literary and artistic sources describe banquets, festivities and royal visits.

The figs of the rich, like most other fine fruits, generally find their historical sources in literary and artistic form, rather than in recipes or account books – although the Portuguese figs offered to Henry VIII and specially recorded in his privy purse accounts give us one evocative source.

The Figs of the Poor

Sources of information about the food of the poor are fewer. There can be some extrapolation from account books of poorhouses, prisons and hospitals, but many sources are perforce more impressionistic. Food historians have to draw upon travellers' tales, passing references and popular writings such as nursery rhymes.

Historical proverbs are some of the best sources for learning about popular foods; in the best and most genuine proverbs in all languages we can hear the historical voice of the poor and the oppressed talking about their diet, usually expressing a folk wisdom or a set of beliefs which belong in the period up to and including the fifteenth century.

The Oxford English Dictionary cites Dr South (1634–1716) giving a strong view of the value of proverbs: 'What is a proverb, but the experience and observation of several ages, gathered and summed up into one expression.' The same idea was expressed in a pejorative way by Lord Chesterfield, who advised his son that proverbs were 'the rhetoric of the vulgar man' and should be avoided by men of fashion. The greatest authority on proverbs (or paremiologist), Archer Taylor, on several occasions indicated his belief that proverbs reflect the interest and the world of the common people.

When we look for fig proverbs, we immediately find that the English language is not much help. Figs played almost no part in British popular culture in medieval and pre-medieval times, and as a result there are hardly any British proverbs about figs as a food. Figs do find their way into phrase and fable, however, by analogy, in popular and vulgar phrases such as 'not worth a fig' and 'don't give a fig'.

The expression 'not worth a fig' existed in ancient Greek (it is found in Athenaeus, despite his great love of figs), and now exists in many languages, notably in Turkish, where the movie *İncir Çekirdeği* (*Not Worth a Fig*, directed by Selda Çiçek, 2009) is regarded as a new landmark in Turkish cinema. It finds its way into several memorable Spanish proverbs:

> *Amigo sin dinero, eso quiero; que dinero sin amigo no vale un higo.*
> A friend without money, that I love; money without a friend is not worth a fig.

> *Blanca con frio no vale un higo.*
> A fair woman in cold weather is not worth a fig.

> *Oficio que no da trigo no vale un higo.*
> Trade which provides no wheat is not worth a fig.

The 'not worth a fig' expression is less widely used in French than in Spanish, it would seem, but nonetheless striking phrases do appear in the literature. Two notable and recurrent examples are *La vie ne vaut pas une figue* (Life is not worth a fig) and *Ton amour ne vaut pas une figue* (Your love is not worth a fig).

English and Irish examples are also less common, and some turn out to be Spanish proverbs in translation, but here are four: 'For what is out of date is not worth a fig'; 'His knowledge of human nature is not worth a fig'; 'Satan's kingdom is not worth a fig'; 'The world is not worth a fig (and I have good raisins for saying so)'.

Alongside 'not worth a fig' sits the second common and disparaging phrase referencing our lovely fruit, namely 'don't give a fig'. A well-known early variant of this is used by Shakespeare in Henry v, when Pistol says to Fluellen: 'Die and be damn'd; and figo for thy friendship!' Less well known, but equally memorable and a personal favourite, is the couplet from the *Towneley Mysteries* (as early as 1420): 'A fig for care and a fig for woe! If I can't pay, why I can owe!' Here again the fig seems to be being used as a synonym for something worth nothing at all. Eric Partridge, however, our supreme authority on slang and catchphrases, goes further, and links 'not giving a fig' to the obscene gesture produced by pushing the thumb up between the fingers, described in many languages as a fig gesture, with strong sexual connotations – more common in Italian (*far la fica*) or in French (*faire la figue*) than in English in present times but strongly suggesting that historically 'don't give a fig' was a euphemism for 'don't give a fuck'.

For figs as food, there are wonderful proverbs too, again coming, naturally enough, from the Mediterranean and Levantine countries. While there are hardly any English proverbs about the eating of figs, as we have begun to see, Spain provides many evocative fig proverbs.

For the time of ripening, we find: *Por San Miguel, los higos son miel* (for St Michael, figs are honey-sweet; St Michael's day is 29 September). Figs are the latest of all fruit to ripen. We could also mention here a Lebanese proverb: 'Eat the first cucumbers and the last figs.' Meanwhile, there is a powerful Spanish proverb on perishability, of figs and human beings: *Los hombres somos como los higos: el que no cae hoy cae mañana* (We men are like figs; those who don't die today will die tomorrow).

Using the fig as a symbol of transience in this way is ancient. The Stoic philosopher Epictetus (d. AD 135) sternly told his followers:

> Remind yourself that the one you love is mortal, that what you love does not belong to you; it is given you for the present time, not irrevocably or for ever, but just like a fig or a bunch of grapes at their season of ripeness.

One strange Spanish proverb, recorded by Gonzalo Correas in 1627, appears to refer to the laxative benefits of the fig: *Higo hinchón para mi señor, higo maduro para mi kulo* (Hard green fig for my master; ripe fig for my bum).

Spanish proverbs also refer to the abundance of figs: *Al tiempo de higo, no hay enemigo* (At fig-time, there are no enemies [because there is food for everyone]); while a resonant proverb tells us that fig trees need to mature, although not to the same extent as olive trees: *Olivares de tu abuelo; higueras de tu padre, y viñas de ti mismo* (Your grandfather's olive trees; your father's fig trees; your own vineyards).

There is one (rare) English proverb, collected in the *Book of Meery Riddles* (1629), which appears to confirm the high status of the fig, and which might be of southern European origin: 'Provide a fig for thy friend, and a peach for thine enemy.'

The foods found in proverbs are most often, quite literally, down to earth (onions, leeks, carrots, garlic) and everyday (bread, pies, puddings, apples), and figs sit rather strangely in the corpus of proverbs, because in the hierarchies of foods, and especially the hierarchies of grown products – fruit, cereals, vegetables – the fig belongs right at the top, whereas most proverbial foods belong right at the bottom.

These food hierarchies were especially important in the late medieval period, when the food of the rich and the food of the poor were rigidly separated, as the proverbs themselves repeatedly recognized. If we consider the example of one well-known English proverb – 'leeks are the asparagus of the poor' – it leads us to clear social implications and social distinctions. A high-ranking person would be mortified and insulted to be offered a dish of leeks. A poor person would not aspire to eat asparagus, and would often believe such food to be badly adapted for the digestion of poor people. Better to stick to leeks.

The criteria in the food hierarchies included scarcity value and perishability (key criteria for the food of the rich), but also, strangely, proximity to the soil. The lowest ranked foods are in the dirt; the highest are on the tops of the trees.

The French historian Bruno Laurioux has produced a fascinating table of high- and low-ranking medieval foods. The lowest of all are classed as bulbs (onions, shallots, leeks and garlic). Next lowest are the roots (carrots, turnips, beets). Immediately above the roots in the hierarchy come those leaves which are perceived to spring from roots (spinach, chard, lettuce), and then above these come leaves which grow upon a stem (cabbage, peas, mint). The next rank up features berries and fruits which grow on a bush, and at the top of the plant hierarchy come the fruit which grow on a tree – the nearer to heaven, the more adapted for upper-class food. There was a similar hierarchy for meat, which need not detain us in detail, but which showed pigs at the bottom (nearest to the earth in their habits) and small birds (larks, thrushes, buntings) at the very top.

The fig, growing way up in the tree and very perishable, was ranked more highly than any other fruit or vegetable in the countries of northern Europe, where it also had a high scarcity value. Figs ranked even above dates, because, although dates grow higher in the tree, figs are so much more perishable.

In southern Europe, the status of the fig was ambivalent. Southern figs were paradoxical: so commonplace as to be worthless, so exotically delicate as to be a gift fit for a king; a food adored by peasants, a food of such elevated status as to deserve a place on the finest tables.

The paradox is explained in various ways. The first explanation lies in the two forms of the edible fig: fresh and dried. The fresh fig is an archetypal luxury food because of its perishability; it can be sublime one day and rotten the next. The true exquisiteness of flavour (which is enhanced by pure

Dried figs looking their best, arranged like basketware.

water) belongs only to the fresh fig on its day of perfect ripeness. By contrast, the dried fig is durable – a cheap source of summer sweetness all through the winter, and an ideal staple food.

The second explanation of the paradox is geographical. Figs grow easily and copiously in Mediterranean and Levantine lands, but are exotic imports to northern Europe. Figs grown to the north of, say, Bordeaux or Bologna never have that taste of the southern sun, and this is what led the prophet Muhammad to say: 'If I should wish a fruit brought to paradise, it would certainly be the fig.'

Despite their omnipresence in the Mediterranean region, figs retain their exotic status – touched by strange stories from the Bible, by references in the Koran, by memories of the Crusades and the Ottoman wars. In more recent ideas of gastronomy, they have added a form of exoticism by association. For example, the combination of figs and Parma ham is often described as a marriage made in heaven, while the French have sustained the Roman tradition of giving special status to *foie gras* from geese fed on figs.

In his wonderful book about the relationship between pears and cheese, *Il formaggio con le pere* (2008), the Italian historian Massimo Montanari provides us with further thoughts about both proverbs and the shifting status of the foods of the rich and the foods of the poor.

Montanari's starting point is an Italian proverb which advises: 'Don't let the peasant know how well cheese accompanies pears' (*Al contadino non far sapere quanto è buono il formaggio con le pere*). This leads him to a series of reflections on the exclusiveness of the food of the rich and on specialness, illuminated by Italian proverbs.

For the fig, one of the proverbs he cites is *Al fico l'acqua, e alla pera il vino* (Drink water with figs and wine with pears),

Figs and Parma ham.

with a Campanian variant, *Con i fichi l'acqua, e con le pesche il vino* (Drink water with figs and wine with peaches).

These proverbs place figs in the tradition of luxurious foods which do not take wine, but are enhanced by water – such as artichokes and asparagus. And we should remember that clean drinking water itself was a luxury product in medieval times.

Montanari stresses how difficult it was for peasant foods to be accepted at the tables of the rich. In order for this to happen there had to be, in his terminology, 'strategies' for making the peasant food different, special and hence acceptable. He uses in particular examples from among cheeses and fruits. Mushrooms provide another example (classed as food from dirt, even food from excrement, when eaten by the poor; irresistibly earthily delicious in exotic forms such as *cèpes*). Salt cod (*bacalao*), as mentioned, has a similar ambiguity (the *brandade de morue* is a peasant dish still found in backstreet French cafés, but also an exquisite mix of flavours found in all the aristocratic cookbooks from Escoffier onwards). Cheese, soft fruit, fungus food, salt cod: these are foods of the common people, folk foods, everyday foods, which have such tempting characteristics of deliciousness that the rich need to reclassify them and make them special so that they can grace their own tables.

Forms of specialness could include perishability; delicacy and exquisite subtlety of flavour (too subtle to be appreciated

Diced figs and cheese.

Walter Crane's celebrated *Fig and Peacock* wallpaper of 1895 encircles the beauty of the peacock with the elegance of fig leaves.

At market in all their glory.

by crude peasant palates); having a short season; having exotic origins; and exceptional individual characteristics.

Fresh figs are seasonal, perishable and delicate; they are not quite ripe on a Monday, at their perfect best on a Tuesday, and beginning to collapse on a Wednesday. Although the flavour of figs continues to be excellent when they are over-ripe, for their appearance on aristocratic tables they must be served on their perfect day. We recall Ischomachus' advice to Socrates: although the peasants might harvest a whole tree at one session, and take away up to 10,000 fruit, for the aristocracy the figs should be picked fruit by fruit on the basis of individual ripeness and perfection.

In northern Europe, fresh figs are exotic: Portuguese figs made a regal gift to Henry VIII. In this respect they can sit on aristocratic tables alongside fruits which have no European folk traditions attached, such as pineapples.

Even in countries where fresh figs are abundant, they are treated as supremely special. In Istanbul in August and September the contrast between delicate finesse, on the one hand, and sheer abundance, on the other, is seen to the full. Although fresh figs are sold in the bazaars for less than half the price per kilo of dried figs, they are displayed with as much care and precision as if they were of antique glass. And sold with love and reverence, as befits a divine festive fruit.

Recipes

The following recipes have been chosen from as wide a range of fig-loving countries as possible. The intention is to show how the fig has been adopted into a variety of cuisines worldwide, but also to show how figs can match and partner an astonishing variety of other foods. Some readers, and in particular some of the author's Lebanese friends, will maintain that the fig should be eaten fresh and accompanied only by a glass of arak or other aniseed drink. Similarly, the thesis of David Tanis's delightful book *A Platter of Figs and Other Recipes* (2008) is that some foods are too good to mess with and that a simple platter of perfect figs is the finest of all desserts. Other favourite ways of serving, including candied green figs and fresh figs poached in red wine, are simple enough to need no recipe. Perhaps some of the recipes below will tempt even my Lebanese friends and family to review their position.

Historical Recipes

Here are two authentic medieval recipes for dried figs, from the fifteenth-century *Curye on Inglysch*:

Rapey

Take half figs and half raisins; pike them and wash them in water. Scald them in wine, bray them in a mortar, and draw them through a strainer. Cast them in a pot and therewith powder of pepper and other good powders; allay it up with flour of rice, and colour it with saunders. Salt it, seethe it and mess it forth.

For a modernized version, soak the figs in water before stewing them in red wine; use a blender instead of a mortar and strainer; use cinnamon and nutmeg for the powders; use cornflour for rice flour; and take 'saunders' to mean saffron.

Tourtelettes

Take figs and grind them small; do therein saffron and powder fort. Close them in foils of dough, and fry them in oil. Clarify honey and flame them therewith; eat them hot or cold.

For a modernized version, soak the figs before mincing them and soak the saffron; make the 'powder fort' from cloves and nutmeg, with a little sugar and black pepper; with the clarified honey, use some of the fig water and saffron water to moisten the mixture; and wrap in filo pastry before frying.

Modern Recipes

Menorcan Tomato Soup with Figs

600 g ripe tomatoes
1 green pepper
1 large onion
5 tablespoons olive oil
2 heads garlic
1 ¼ litres water
4 slices of bread
2 sprigs parsley
1 teaspoon sea salt
12 fresh figs

Cut the tomatoes, onion, garlic and pepper into fairly small pieces and put into a *tià* (Menorcan clay pot) or similar. Simmer gently for 25–30 minutes, adding teaspoons of water from time to time. When the mixture is stewed, carefully add the rest of the water, heat slowly and continue to simmer without boiling or bubbling. When the soup is hot and a white foam is starting to form, remove from the heat. Place broken pieces of bread at the bottom of each bowl, cover with soup, and serve with peeled fresh figs.
Serves 6–8

Duck with Honey and Figs

2 duck legs
salt and black pepper
finely grated zest of an orange and a lemon, plus the juice of the orange
a piece of ginger
3 tablespoons honey
6 fresh figs, halved

Preheat the oven to 200°C/400°F. Season the duck legs with salt and black pepper. Fry them carefully in a non-stick frying-pan, for 7–8 minutes, until they just start to brown (there should be no need to add oil; duck should baste itself). Turn the duck legs and cook the other side in the same way.

Put the zest of the orange and lemon in a bowl. Peel the ginger and grate it into the bowl. Pour in the honey and season lightly with salt.

Place the duck legs in a small roasting tin or baking dish, coat with the seasoned honey mixture and roast for 20 minutes. Remove the duck from the oven and pour over the reserved juice of the orange. Place the halved figs around the duck and return to the oven. Continue roasting for a further 10 minutes, or until there are no signs of blood on a testing skewer.

Serves 2

Corsican Anchoiade

6 salted anchovy fillets
8 fresh figs, very ripe
1 clove garlic
olive oil

Wash the salt from the anchovies and peel the figs. Pound the anchovies, figs and garlic with a pestle, drizzling olive oil to obtain a firm paste consistency. Serve on warm fresh bread.

Salade Pleine Forme au Vinaigre de Figues

180 g rice
50 g dried apricots
3 dried figs
1 small cucumber
2 oranges
3 young carrots

bunch of chives
1 teaspoon honey
1 teaspoon cumin
4 tablespoons olive oil
3 tablespoons fig vinegar*
handful of unsalted pistachios

*The fig vinegar should not be balsamic, but the sort of fruit vinegar available, for example, from A L'Olivier of Nice.

Cook and drain the rice. Squeeze the oranges. Peel the carrots and cut into cubes. Cook the carrots as gently as possibly for 12 minutes in the orange juice, with the cumin and the honey. Drip in teaspoons of water to keep the mixture liquid. Cut the figs and apricots into small pieces and add them to the mixture. Set aside to cool. Peel and core the cucumber and cut into small pieces. Mix the cucumber into the rice, and then add the compote of carrots and fruit. Season with olive oil and fig vinegar; salt and pepper to taste. Sprinkle with pistachios and chopped chives, and serve. *Serves 4*

Fettuccine with Figs, Chard and Gorgonzola

250 g fettuccine
8 fresh figs, quartered
8–10 leaves chard, stems removed, leaves torn
2 tablespoons olive oil
2 cloves garlic, minced
75 g Gorgonzola, crumbled
½ tablespoon balsamic vinegar
1 handful walnut pieces

Cook fettuccine according to directions. Heat 1 tablespoon olive oil in a pan and gently fry the minced garlic (without letting it brown). Add the torn chard leaves and cook over medium heat until just starting to wilt.

Add the cooked pasta, 1 tablespoon olive oil, Gorgonzola and balsamic vinegar into the chard. Stir well and toss in walnut pieces. Decorate with the fig quarters.

Serves 4

Insalatina di Scampi, Fichi e Melone

600 g fat prawns
4 plum tomatoes
6 white figs
1 melon
half a grapefruit
half a lemon
handful of rocket leaves
Tabasco to taste
good quality olive oil to taste
salt and pepper to taste

Cook and shell the prawns. Leave to cool. Peel the tomatoes and remove the seeds. Mix the tomato flesh with the flesh of the grapefruit, lemon juice, Tabasco, salt, pepper and olive oil. Set aside. Use a melon scoop to create melon balls. Peel and quarter the figs. Serve the salad on a large flat plate, in circles: the rocket at the centre, surrounded by a circle of prawns, a circle of figs, and a circle of melon balls on the outside. Dress with the tomato and grapefruit mixture, teaspoon by teaspoon.

Serves 4

Griddled Figs with Prosciutto

12 fresh figs
12 slices prosciutto
balsamic vinegar to taste
salt and pepper to taste

Cut the figs in half lengthways. Heat a griddle pan, and when very hot place figs face-down in the pan and char (1–2 minutes). Remove to a serving dish; place each fig charred side up; drizzle with balsamic vinegar; add salt and pepper; curl a piece of prosciutto around each fig; and rush to the table while the figs are still warm.

Serves 4

Turkish Fig Sherbet

4 dried figs
¾ litre water
50 ml pekmez*

*Pekmez is a thick syrup obtained by condensing grape must. If pekmez cannot be found, use caster sugar (4 or 5 tablespoons).

Boil the figs for 30 minutes, until they are really falling apart. Strain through a colander, reserving the liquid; then push through a strainer and finally through a fine sieve, again reserving the liquid. Add a little more water to the fig liquid and return to the heat; bring to a boil, then remove from the heat until cool. Add the pekmez or sugar; return to the heat and bring back to the boil. Again remove from the heat and cool. Pour into glasses, chill, and serve decorated with fresh mint.

Serves 4

İncir Tatlisi (Turkish stuffed figs baked in rose syrup)

12 dried figs
caster sugar
rose water to taste
handful of walnuts

Soak the figs in hot water until they are soft and plump. Cut the stem from each fig and carefully stuff with crushed walnuts and a little sugar. In a large shallow pan put half an inch of water flavoured with rose water and sugar. Gently poach the figs until the rose syrup is absorbed. Leave to cool. Serve decorated with cream and walnut halves.

Serves 4

Figgy Pudding

24 dried figs
120 ml brandy
50 g self-raising flour
1 teaspoon freshly grated nutmeg
½ teaspoon cinnamon
100 g shredded vegetarian suet
175 g breadcrumbs
200 g chopped dates
75 g raisins
1 orange, zest and juice only
juice of small piece of root ginger
2 eggs

Put the figs in a bowl and add the brandy. Cover and leave overnight, then drain (reserving the brandy) and chop the figs into small pieces.

In a second bowl, mix together the flour, nutmeg, cinnamon, suet, breadcrumbs, dates and raisins.

In a third bowl, whisk together the reserved brandy, orange zest and juice, the juice from the ginger, and the eggs, until all well combined.

Add the brandy mixture into the flour mixture and mix well to combine, until smooth. Stir in the figs, then spoon the mixture into a pudding dish and cover with buttered greaseproof paper followed by a pudding cloth. Secure well with kitchen string.

Steam in a large pan of water for about four hours, topping up the water as required, until the pudding is cooked through and firm.

Unwrap, and serve the pudding in slices with custard.

Serves 6–8

Select Bibliography

On Figs

Condit, Ira J., *The Fig* (Waltham, MA, 1947)

—, 'Fig History in the New World', *Agricultural History*, XXXI/2 (April 1957), pp. 19–24

Fuster, Xim, et al., *Minorca: Cooking and Gastronomy* (Sant Lluís, 2005)

Henry, Diana, *Roast Figs, Sugar Snow: Food to Warm the Soul* (London, 2005)

Loohuizen, Ria, *The Realm of Fig and Quince*, trans. Alissa Valles (Totnes, 2010)

Meijer, F. J., 'Cato's African Figs', *Mnemosyne*, XXXVII (1984), pp. 117–24

Phillips, Henry, *The Companion for the Orchard: An Historical and Botanical Account of Fruits Known in Great Britain* (London, 1831)

Simmons, Marie, *Fig Heaven: 70 Recipes for the World's Most Luscious Fruit* (New York, 2004)

Storey, W. B., 'Figs', in *Advances in Fruit Breeding*, ed. Jules Janick and James N. Moore (West Lafayette, IN, 1975), pp. 568–89

Sutton, David C., 'The Festive Fruit: A History of Figs', in *Celebrations: Proceedings of the Oxford Symposium on Food and Cookery 2011*, ed. Mark McWilliams (Totnes, 2012), pp. 335–45

Tanis, David, *A Platter of Figs, and Other Recipes* (New York, 2008)

Other Works

Flandrin, Jean-Louis, and Massimo Montanari, eds, *Histoire de l'alimentation* (Paris, 1996)

Flowerdew, Bob, *The Gourmet Gardener* (London, 2005)

Gürsoy, Denis, *Turkish Cuisine in Historical Perspective* (Istanbul, 2006)

Laurioux, Bruno, *Manger au Moyen Âge: pratiques et discours alimentaires en Europe au XIVe et XVe siècles* (Paris, 2002)

Montanari, Massimo, *La fame e l'abbondanza: storia dell'alimentazione in Europa* (Rome, 1994)

—, *Il formaggio con le pere: la storia in un proverbio* (Bari, 2008)

Riley, Gillian, *The Oxford Companion to Italian Food* (Oxford, 2007)

Sutton, David C., 'The Stories of Bacalao: Myth, Legend and History', in *Cured, Fermented and Smoked Foods: Proceedings of the Oxford Symposium on Food and Cookery 2010*, ed. Helen Saberi (Totnes, 2011), pp. 312–21

Thirsk, Joan, *Food in Early Modern England: Phases, Fads, Fashions, 1500–1760* (London, 2007)

Websites and Associations

California Figs
www.californiafigs.com

California Rare Fruit Growers
www.crfg.org

Festa di u Ficu, Peri, Corsica
www.festadiuficu.com

Fig Recipes
www.figrecipes.co.uk

Figs for Fun Forum
www.figs4fun.com

Figueres pròpies dels països catalans i del meu terrat
www.galgoni.com

Figweb (via Iziko Museums of Cape Town)
www.figweb.org

A Modern Herbal
www.botanical.com

North American Fruit Explorers
www.nafex.org

Royal Horticultural Society
www.rhs.org.uk

San Joaquin Figs, Inc.
www.nutrafig.com

Le Syndicat de Défense de la Figue de Solliès
www.figue.org

Acknowledgements

This book developed from a presentation on the history of figs given at the Oxford Symposium on Food and Cookery. I am grateful to Michael Leaman for suggesting that the presentation could be expanded into a volume in Reaktion Books' Edible Series, and for all his help thereafter. I have been helped by colleagues at the Oxford Symposium, especially Paul Levy; and by former colleagues on the Histoire de l'Alimentation course formerly led by Jean-Louis Flandrin at the Université de Paris-VIII. I am especially grateful to Jeanne Allard and Pedro Cantero in Seville; Esther Cruces Blanco in Malaga; Christine Martinez and her family in Paris and Toulouse; Cathy Henderson in Austin, Texas; and Trish Thomas, Daniela La Penna and Deborah Jenkins in Reading, England.

Photo Acknowledgements

The author and publishers wish to express their thanks to the below sources of illustrative material and/or permission to reproduce it. Some locations of artworks are also given below.

Photo abracadabra99/BigStockPhoto: p. 85; photo Alinari/ Rex Features: p. 51; photos © Alinari/Roger-Viollet, courtesy Rex Features: pp. 65, 68; photo photoarchive.saudiaramcoworld.com: p. 66; photo assalve/iStock International: p. 30; photo BasPhoto/ BigStockPhoto: p. 41 (top); British Museum, London (photos © the Trustees of the British Museum): pp. 19, 20, 38, 41 (foot); Brussels Cathedral: p. 63; photo cristiacio/BigStockPhoto: p. 107; photo CSU Archives/Everett Collection/Rex Features: p. 47; photo cynoclub/BigStockPhoto: p. 50; photo DEA/M. Cerri/UIG/Rex Features: p. 26; photo dibrova/iStock International: p. 27; photo DNY59/iStock International: p. 11; photo Food and Drink/Rex Features: pp. 14, 83; photo illu/BigStockPhoto: p. 8; photos Image Broker/Rex Features: pp. 10 (top), 28, 94; photos Deborah Jenkins: pp. 32, 73; photo jjspring/BigStockPhoto: p. 102; photo Jorisvo/ BigStockPhoto: p. 63; photo Henryk T. Kaiser/Rex Features: p. 71; photos Rozenn Leboucher/Rex Features: pp. 34, 39; photo Lehner/ iStock International: p. 86; Library of Congress, Washington, DC (Prints and Photographs Division): p. 37; Musée du Louvre, Paris: p. 10 (foot); Museo de Bellas Artes, Seville: p. 96; National Library of Austria, Vienna: pp. 65, 68; photo nito/BigStockPhoto: p. 105; PerseoMedusa/BigStockPhoto: p. 16; private collection: p. 15; photo

Index

italic numbers refer to illustrations; **bold** to recipes